MODERN
MEDITERRANEAN

MODERN
MEDITERRANEAN
EASY, FLAVORFUL HOME COOKING

MELIA MARDEN

EXECUTIVE CHEF, THE SMILE

PHOTOGRAPHS BY LUCY SCHAEFFER

STEWART, TABORI & CHANG | NEW YORK

Published in 2013 by Stewart, Tabori & Chang
An imprint of ABRAMS

Text copyright © 2013 Melia Marden
Photographs copyright © 2013 Lucy Schaeffer

Library of Congress Cataloging-in-Publication Data

Marden, Melia.
 Modern Mediterranean / Melia Marden.
    pages cm
 Includes bibliographical references.
 ISBN 978-1-61769-018-1
1. Cooking, Mediterranean. I. Title.
 TX725.M35M384 2013
 641.59182'2--dc23
                              2012036375

EDITOR: Natalie Kaire
DESIGNER: Laura Palese
MANAGING EDITOR: Jen Graham
PRODUCTION MANAGER: True Sims
FOOD STYLING: Simon Andrews
PROP STYLING: Amy Wilson

The text of this book was composed in Neutra and Futura.

Printed and bound in China

10 9 8 7 6 5 4 3 2 1

Stewart, Tabori & Chang books are available at special discounts
when purchased in quantity for premiums and promotions as well as
fundraising or educational use. Special editions can also be created
to specification. For details, contact specialsales@abramsbooks.com
or the address below.

ABRAMS
THE ART OF BOOKS SINCE 1949
115 West 18th Street
New York, NY 10011
www.abramsbooks.com

THE OLD FERRY that you used to take from Athens (long since replaced by higher-speed hydrofoils)

CON-
TEN-
TS

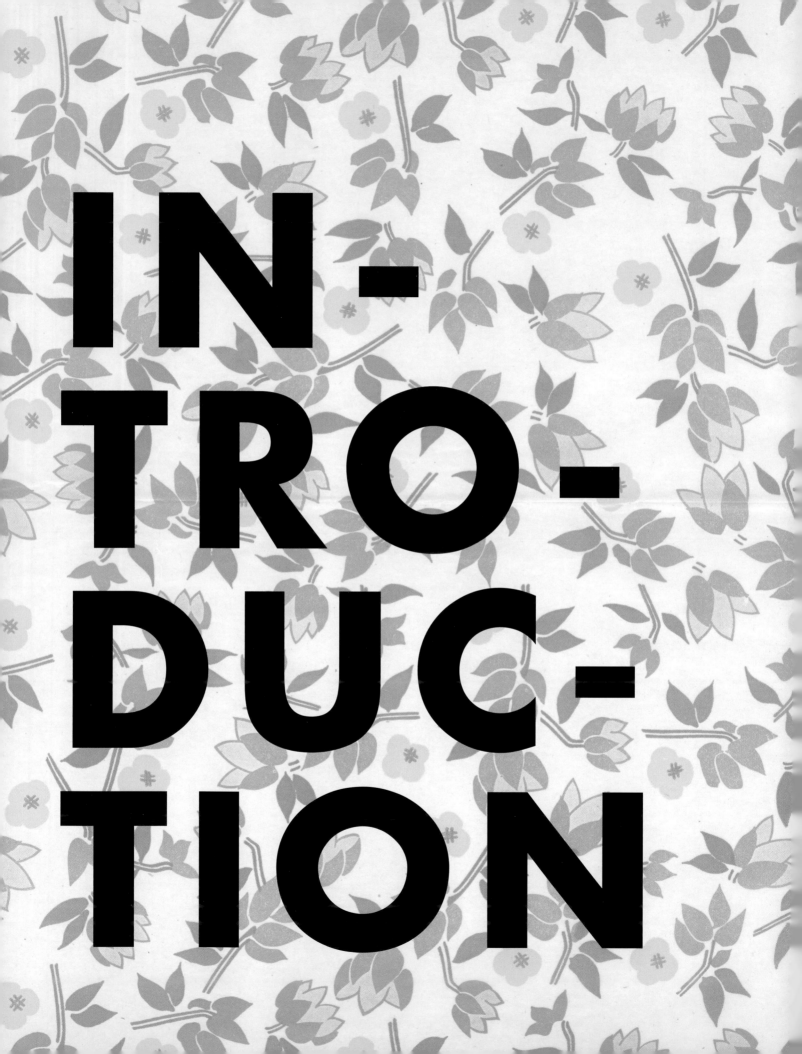

IN-
TRO-
DUC-
TION

I WOULDN'T BE A PROFESSIONAL CHEF TODAY IF IT WEREN'T FOR MY MOTHER, not only because she was an amazing cook, but also because she created a life for her family in which delicious food was a constant, valued presence. Throughout her life she had an innate urge to travel. She spent her childhood in Williamsport, Pennsylvania, and as soon as she graduated from college she took a summer job as a flight attendant on a small charter airline, flying to Europe and North Africa. Skip ahead to the 1970s. After moving to New York City and meeting my father, her lifelong wanderlust led her to the small rocky island of Hydra, Greece. Though only two hours from Athens, Hydra seems to belong to another time: A strictly enforced law prohibits any kind of car or vehicle; donkeys, wooden fishing boats, and now water taxis provide the main forms of transportation. Drawn to the eccentric community of foreigners living cheaply in this idyllic, sun-drenched landscape, my mother decided to make Hydra a permanent part of her life. She returned with my father the next year, eventually buying an old farmhouse in the hills of Kamini, four hundred winding stone steps up from the main port.

I've been lucky enough to spend almost every summer of my life in that house. During falls and winters in New York City, I would dream about the rustic island cooking at Hydra's pristine seafront tavernas—perfectly charred whole fish and rosemary-rubbed lamb chops right off the grill, intensely sweet red onions with ripe tomatoes topped with tangy feta, and delicately fried zucchini dipped in potent, garlicky *tzatziki*. Returning to Hydra every year was like a culinary homecoming; I never tired of its food, even after weeks of crisp salads and grilled fish. It was there that I internalized the hallmark of great Mediterranean cooking, a kind of simplicity that's perfectly balanced—the flavors of clean, fresh ingredients playing off one another so that you are able to taste everything at once.

Back home in New York, I was fortunate enough to grow up surrounded by a vibrantly international culinary culture—the Greek tavernas in Astoria echoing my experiences on Hydra with their grilled red snapper and lemony olive oil; the Moroccan spices and fresh kaffir-lime leaves at specialty groceries like Kalustyan's in Murray Hill; and the family-run Italian shops in Greenwich Village selling handmade mozzarella, fresh tortellini, and crushed tomatoes. Sometime in the early 1980s, my mom took a Moroccan cooking class with the now legendary cookbook author Paula Wolfert. The influence of that class and subsequent trips to Morocco formed the backbone of our family meals. Our traditional Christmas dinner became a deliciously aromatic chicken, preserved lemon, and cracked green olive tagine, accompanied by a giant bowl of fluffy couscous topped with simmered winter vegetables. If Greek food can be characterized by the bold saltiness of olives and capers, Moroccan food has the darker, earthier sweetness of dates, cinnamon-scented onions, and preserved lemons. Without realizing it, I was developing the tastes that would shape my cooking for years to come.

MY MOM on a picnic boat (mid-'90s)

Like many people, I loved food without ever seriously considering it as a profession. Cooking seemed like the backdrop of my life, not the center. I went to college, studied art history, and found myself with a post-graduation sense of aimlessness. But as with so many things in life, the answer I was looking for was right in front of me. While assisting part time at a magazine, I did background research on up-and-coming chefs for an article about "the next Martha Stewart" (she had just been found guilty of insider trading and was heading to prison). I felt a rising sense of jealousy that these people were doing something so directly gratifying, working with their hands, creating delicious food that could be instantly appreciated. Having had no professional cooking experience, and not a lot of amateur experience either, I immediately enrolled in culinary school. Six months later, my friend Meredith and I started a company called Looking Glass Catering, booking jobs through friends and cooking out of a kitchen the size of a bathtub in my apartment on East Tenth Street. At that point, we were making it up as we went along. I took other food-related jobs as well—working as a private chef for a family, interning at a fledgling food magazine, and assisting a food writer with recipe testing. Right from the beginning, I never looked back; I loved that cooking had become my world and that I was interacting with it every day. Fortunately, I still love having a job that allows me to never stop learning. Every time I eat somewhere new or try something different, I can be inspired by ingredients, techniques, and combinations that had never occurred to me before.

In 2008 my friend Carlos asked me to check out his new project, a café on the ground floor of a historic 1830s Bond Street townhouse, just one block away from my apartment in New York. Coincidentally, it was the first building my parents had lived in together after they got married. It must have been a sign, as one thing led to another and, soon after, Carlos and his business partner, Matt, asked me to design the menu and be the executive chef at The Smile. None of us had ever run a restaurant; I myself had just barely worked in one before, and only for a few months. The building was old and had obviously never been designed for any kind of food operation. The kitchen was awkward and tiny, with no ventilation or gas hookup. In the end, the limitations helped me create a more personal, low-key menu of foods that felt home cooked and that fit with the relaxed atmosphere of the space. While we learned a few things the hard way (not having air-conditioning in August that first year was definitely a low point), eventually everything fell into place.

When customers and friends ask what kind of food we serve at The Smile, I've settled on describing it as "Manhattan Mediterranean." The phrase is meant to encompass the flavorful cooking of Greece and Morocco, coastal Italy, Spain, and southern France, combined with the melting-pot atmosphere of New York and the fresh local produce that continues to inspire my seasonally changing menus. I like to think that you don't have to live in New York City for this idea to be relevant. To me, it's about synthesizing

The walk down to the port from my parents' house in the HILLS OF KAMINI

your favorite food experiences into a cooking style that makes sense for you. While my heart belongs to Mediterranean cooking, my day-to-day experience is grounded in my home and my restaurant in New York—the seasons, the changing produce at the farmers' market, the family-run purveyors that I work with every day. Naturally my cooking reflects all of that, as well as the constant inspiration I get from the seemingly endless variety of restaurants around the city.

The first review of The Smile summed up my food as "influenced by her mother's eclectic, informal dinner parties" and went on to say that I cooked like an "especially talented dinner-party hostess, re-creating taste memories of places she's been and dishes she's loved." I have a feeling that some chefs would be insulted by that description, preferring not to be compared to an amateur throwing a dinner party. To me, the description perfectly captured what I want out of being a chef. My goal is to make food that doesn't taste like you're eating in a restaurant; I want customers to feel the unique comfort and pure pleasure of being served a great home-cooked meal, that feeling my mom created for her family and friends for so many years.

I didn't inherit my mother's natural affinity for travel and adventure; at heart, I'm a homebody who finds nothing more satisfying than retreating into her own kitchen. However, I am motivated by a desire to eat, to try new things, and to experience all the delicious food that the world has to offer. A recent road trip through Provence with my husband reestablished my faith in the sublime quality of simply prepared fresh Mediterranean cooking. A lunch of grilled trout seasoned only with toasted fennel seeds, salt, and pepper was one of the best meals I've ever had. With this cookbook I want to share what I've learned from those kinds of experiences. These are the fresh seasonal recipes I've gathered over many summers in Hydra, while traveling throughout the Mediterranean, and while honing my skills in New York kitchens.

Though I certainly don't think I'm qualified to write the definitive book on Greek or Moroccan cooking, I hope that I can convey my genuine love of Mediterranean cuisine as it is reflected in these recipes. Ultimately, this book is a celebration of flavor and food culture: the bright, clean flavors of sea salt, citrus, olive oil, fresh herbs, ripe tomatoes, and crisp watermelon, and the earthy richness of plums, figs, dates, caramelized onions, and roasted meats. I want these recipes to evoke the experience of buying sun-warmed spiced olives from a market stall in Barcelona, the excitement of early-morning trips to the Union Square Greenmarket in spring, and the unique joy of unearthing a new favorite dish at a restaurant hidden in an undiscovered corner of the city. I hope to convey my feeling that cooking can be purely satisfying, and sometimes even transcendent. As the world becomes increasingly fast-paced, it's more important than ever to savor the simple pleasures of creating a good meal.

A PICNIC on a fishing boat, mid-'80s

This book opens with a chapter called "Stocking Up," which is a sort of cheat sheet for building an abundant and exotic Mediterranean pantry. Of course, you don't have to stock your fridge exactly as I stock mine to be able

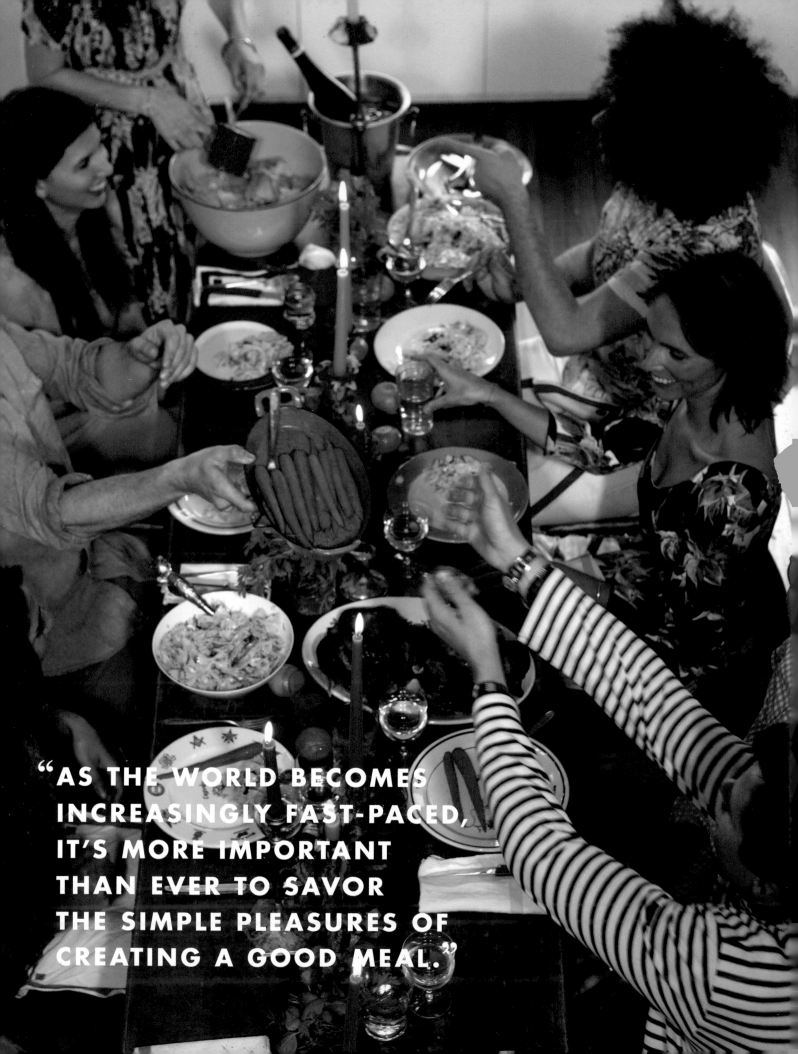

"AS THE WORLD BECOMES INCREASINGLY FAST-PACED, IT'S MORE IMPORTANT THAN EVER TO SAVOR THE SIMPLE PLEASURES OF CREATING A GOOD MEAL."

to cook from these recipes. To give you a sense of what I like to work with, I've laid out a suggested shopping list of a few items: a combination of basics for last-minute dinners and a few harder-to-find products that have become staples in my kitchen. This is followed by a series of easy recipes for snacks and condiments that can be made anytime and kept on hand to add a bit of spice or a burst of flavor, or can function as mini meals unto themselves.

The rest of my recipes are arranged in standard categories. The dishes in "Appetizers & Drinks" are perfect for predinner snacks, light lunches, cocktail parties, and nightcaps. Some of my favorite dishes can be found in the "Salads," "Soups," and "Vegetables & Starches" chapters: Often they're the foods I'll build a meal around, and the recipes I come back to again and again. Within each category I've tried to provide something for every season without being too regimented about it—among the salads, for example, are a lightly dressed mixture of Bibb lettuce and shaved radishes as well as a more substantial frisée salad with crisp bacon, dates, and hard-boiled quail eggs. You can find hearty main-course dishes in "Pizza & Pasta," "Fish," and "Meat & Poultry."

Most of my cooking tends to be on the healthy side, but I'd never call it diet food. I naturally steer away from overpowering the ingredients with tons of butter, heavy sauces, or deep-frying (although sometimes a bit of good-quality butter is exactly what you need to add a touch of richness or balance acidity). These are recipes for meals that will leave you feeling satiated, not soporific.

While I'm not a big-time baker, I do love ending a meal with a final touch of something sweet. I've included dessert recipes that can be thrown together in a few minutes—plums simmered with a vanilla bean and brown sugar, richly spiced hot chocolate poured over strips of orange zest, and almond-scented whipped cream folded into Greek yogurt. If you're feeling a bit more formal and have the time, there are also some more classic baked treats, such as my fluffy lemon and olive oil pound cake and darkly sweet, gingerbread-like sticky-toffee date pudding.

If you're like me, you don't read a cookbook cover to cover but find yourself flipping through it looking for something that catches your eye and then building a meal around that recipe. Or sometimes I'll open a book looking for something specific, an idea for the bunch of kale I bought that morning or a recipe to satisfy my craving for a substantial winter soup. That said, I've provided some sample menus to give you an idea of how I like to pair dishes and flavors. At the end of the day, everything comes together on the plate, and thoughtful consideration of how foods can complement one another will make your meals that much more memorable.

My sister and me (she's on the left) HAVING A PICNIC in the hills behind our house

NOTES ON USING THE RECIPES

Like most people, when I cook at home I don't weigh every tomato or break out my stopwatch to ensure that I've sautéed my onions for exactly one minute. The most natural way to cook is to get a feel for what you want out of every step and to taste for flavor as you go. At the same time, it's incredibly frustrating to follow a recipe and end up with a dish that looks nothing like the photo and just tastes off; you're left wondering if it was you or the writer who missed something. While I've loved and enjoyed cookbooks that list ingredients in a casual way (a dollop of cream, a small bunch of herbs, a good splash of vinegar), I've tried to be as specific as possible here. I've given precise weight measurements where they apply, as well as more intuitive descriptions—for example, 1½ pounds of kale is equal to 3 bunches. Sizes of vegetables vary from market to market, and your butternut squash might be half the size of mine, so to be on the safe side, I've included the weight as well as the volume or quantity.

I have a favorite trick that I use when following someone else's recipe or developing my own: I've measured the top joint of my index finger as approximately 1 inch long. I use this as an easy reference to see if I've got the right thickness when I'm chopping vegetables or cutting meat.

Just as there will be variations in vegetable size, there will be variations from cook to cook: Your oven might be cooler or hotter than mine, your pan a bit wider or deeper or heavier. All these elements affect cooking time and the way that a dish develops. Cooking isn't just a list of instructions but an engagement with the process; I've tried to indicate what you should be seeing and experiencing as you cook (the changing color of caramelized onions, the scent of toasted fennel seeds), along with a suggested cooking time for each step. In my job as an executive chef, I'm constantly fighting a kind of kitchen entropy, the tendency for every cook to gradually veer away from the original idea into doing things his or her own way. While at a restaurant you want the food to taste and look fairly consistent from day to day, the home cook has the advantage of adapting and playing around with recipes. I hope you'll think of the recipes in this book as jumping-off points for your own explorations. I've come up with procedures that work for me, and now you can use the techniques and flavor combinations that you prefer and make each dish your own.

THE ROCKY COAST
of Hydra

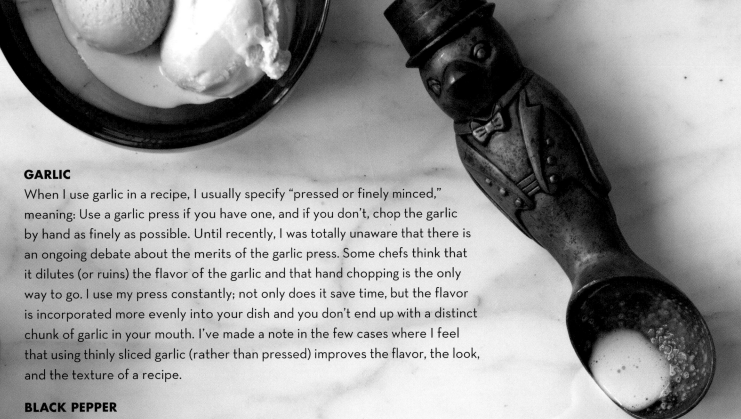

GARLIC

When I use garlic in a recipe, I usually specify "pressed or finely minced," meaning: Use a garlic press if you have one, and if you don't, chop the garlic by hand as finely as possible. Until recently, I was totally unaware that there is an ongoing debate about the merits of the garlic press. Some chefs think that it dilutes (or ruins) the flavor of the garlic and that hand chopping is the only way to go. I use my press constantly; not only does it save time, but the flavor is incorporated more evenly into your dish and you don't end up with a distinct chunk of garlic in your mouth. I've made a note in the few cases where I feel that using thinly sliced garlic (rather than pressed) improves the flavor, the look, and the texture of a recipe.

BLACK PEPPER

Almost every savory recipe in this book includes black pepper in the ingredients list. I've decided against giving a precise measurement for pepper because it seems misleading, given the way I cook. I never use preground black pepper, because you get a cleaner flavor and a nicely varied texture from freshly ground whole peppercorns. I keep a big pepper mill by the stove and give it a few good turns into whatever I'm cooking—I've noted where a more generous amount is recommended. The one exception is my peppery grilled rib eye recipe (see page 186), in which the specific amount of pepper is an essential aspect of the dish.

KOSHER SALT

I confess that before I went to cooking school I didn't really know what kosher salt was. Now I use it almost exclusively in both my home and professional kitchens. Kosher salt has larger and flatter grains than table salt. Because of this, it's easier to grab a pinch with your fingers and to get a tactile sense of how much you're using, allowing you to control your seasoning without measuring. The coarse grains also add a nice textural crunch to roasted meats and vegetables. I've indicated the use of kosher salt in almost all instances, except the baked desserts. Because the kosher salt grains take up more volume by weight, if you are using regular table salt you need to reduce the measurement by roughly half: 1 teaspoon kosher salt would be equivalent to 1/2 teaspoon table salt.

1

STOCKING UP

THE ABUNDANT PANTRY: A SHOPPING LIST

There are certain ingredients that I always come back to, pantry staples I like to have on hand to help me throw together a meal at the last minute. This is a shopping list of the items I usually keep in stock—a combination of classic never-fail basics and exotic products that can liven up a recipe in a pinch.

EXTRA-VIRGIN OLIVE OIL: Can't live without it. The basis for 99 percent of my savory cooking.

KALAMATA OLIVES: I always have a jar in the fridge. Great for giving a quick pasta or pan-seared chicken breast rich, salty flavor.

CRUSHED TOMATOES: During the summer I love to use fresh ripe tomatoes. In the winter, crushed or diced tomatoes are an essential base for pasta sauces, soups, and stews. For some dishes (like my puttanesca sauce and my Moroccan meatballs) I actually prefer the intense flavor you get from the canned variety. My favorite brand is the Italian import Sclafani; to me it has the perfect balance of sweetness, acidity, and saltiness, as well as a good consistency.

YOUR PREFERRED DRIED PASTA: Needs no explanation. When all else fails, you can usually pull together a delicious pasta dish from the contents of your pantry. I always have a box of *penne rigate* on hand for last-minute meals.

CAPERS: Great for sprinkling into sautéed vegetables or over salads for a briny kick.

GRAPE LEAVES IN BRINE: Roughly chopped, they can be used to add a bit of salt and heft to a dish.

RAS EL HANOUT: A North African spice blend that adds a unique warmth to roasted meats, stews, and soups. The ingredients vary but can include cinnamon, cardamom, coriander, nutmeg, chilies, and dried rosebuds.

HARISSA: A fiery Tunisian chili paste, this slightly smoky mixture can be used as a rub for meats, added to marinades or broths, or served alongside dishes as a hot sauce. I buy mine in a bright yellow-and-red tube from a nearby spice shop; every brand I've seen has beautiful illustrated packaging.

PINK PEPPERCORNS: Tender and sweet enough to eat whole, these bright pink young peppercorns make an attractive addition to pickles and salads.

DATE MOLASSES: Darkly sweet and flavorful, like a Middle Eastern version of maple syrup. I use it as a sugar substitute in baking, as in the Sticky-Toffee Date Pudding (page 220), or drizzle it over oatmeal or yogurt for breakfast.

POMEGRANATE SYRUP: This tangy, not-too-sweet syrup has the concentrated taste of fresh pomegranates. Use it to glaze root vegetables such as carrots or parsnips in place of honey, or add a drizzle to balsamic salad dressing. Also terrific poured over baked ham before heating it in the oven.

TRICKS UP YOUR SLEEVE: RECIPES THAT KEEP AND ADVICE ON WHEN TO USE THEM

I find that cooking in the right circumstances can be very relaxing—especially if I'm making a dish I know well and love. There's something about working with my hands and moving through familiar motions that calms me down. Because cooking is such a tactile, physical occupation, it requires that you stay alert; you're involved in a steady rhythm of actions, so you can't be distracted by your day-to-day anxieties. (Granted, I don't always feel this sense of calm when I'm racing to finish my prep for a busy night at the restaurant, or when I've invited ten people over for Christmas dinner and have decided to bake a difficult cake just for the fun of it!) The recipes in this section are the ones I like to make when I feel like cooking without the pressure, when I have a little extra time or just want to be alone in my kitchen.

None of these recipes is difficult or time-consuming, and they can all be used for weeks to come. I like to think of my time in the kitchen preparing these staples as giving my future self a present: pickles that can be added to sandwiches, tossed in salads, or simply nibbled on with a wedge of cheese; or infused salts and sugars that can be sprinkled over food for an extra boost of intense flavor. When fleeting seasonal produce is available, I try to take advantage of it and make it last; a batch of ramp pickles from the spring will last till winter, when it's time to make a jar of Meyer lemon confit. Part of my concept for this chapter is to avoid an all-or-nothing mentality. I don't expect you to be a full-on pioneer, making all your own jam and curing your own meat. Most of us don't have the time, space, or inclination for that. But if you don't have much time to cook one night, it's nice to be able to drizzle your homemade chili oil onto a quickly thrown together pasta dish. Make a big batch of homemade granola and you'll have your breakfast taken care of for weeks. Experiment with some candied pistachios one day and impress friends by crumbling them over a simple bitter-greens salad another. Being a great home cook doesn't have to mean cooking every meal every day or making all your food from scratch. Sometimes it can simply mean putting a little time into preparing ingredients in advance so you can enjoy the fruits of your efforts later, at a leisurely pace.

ALMOND BUTTER

Makes 2 cups (500 grams)

2 cups (286 grams) raw whole almonds

2 teaspoons honey

¼ teaspoon kosher salt

½ cup (120 milliliters) vegetable oil

If you have a food processor, you never need to buy nut butters. The consistency won't be supermarket smooth, but you can really taste the raw freshness of the almonds in this recipe. I like to spread some on toasted multigrain bread with a little bit of honey for a quick, satisfying breakfast or midday snack.

1   Place the almonds, honey, and salt in a food processor and blend until well combined. With the processor running, slowly drizzle in the oil and continue blending until smooth.

2   Store, refrigerated, for up to 1 week. Let the almond butter come to room temperature before using and stir to recombine the oils.

SETTING THE TABLE

The time and effort you need to put into cooking dinner can be daunting, but for me the worst part is undeniably the looming threat of having to clean up at the end of the night. Save yourself some trouble and bring everything to the table in its cooking pot. For hot dishes, place a clean, folded dishtowel or small wooden cutting board on the table first to protect its surface. Of course, this presentation will look a lot better if you use attractive, brightly colored pots and pans. I recommend investing in one medium or large Le Creuset Dutch oven. They come in a variety of beautiful shades and always look great on the table, but they also can improve your cooking: The cast iron heats evenly and helps you to get a rich, flavorful browning on seared meats and vegetables. I also like to use my classic black cast-iron frying pan for sautéed side dishes. You can buy them new or seek out a bargain at secondhand shops or flea markets. Old rusted cast iron can usually be brought back to life with a few tricks; a simple search online turns up countless tutorials. Among my other favorites are vintage enamel Dansk roasting pans and saucepans. I love their clean, minimal design and intense, bright colors. You can find them easily online or at flea markets, and they're usually relatively inexpensive. With a few nice pots and pans, the table always looks festive and, as a bonus, the food will stay warm longer.

ROSE-COLORED APPLESAUCE

Every October a good friend and I celebrate her birthday by going apple-picking upstate at a beautiful orchard set on an expanse of sloping hillside. We always have a great time, eating apples right off the trees and getting a little drunk on cider that we've spiked with bourbon. I invariably end up with a huge bag of apples that I can't finish fast enough slowly rotting on my kitchen table, so I started making this applesauce to put the peak-season fruit to good use. I based the recipe on my mother's two pieces of advice: Don't add a lot of sweetener, since the apples themselves are naturally sweet enough, and throw in a pear and a quince to add an extra dimension of flavor. For a heartier texture and tarter flavor, I leave half the apples unpeeled, and I make sure to use some with pink or red skin to infuse everything with a warm rosy color.

1   Peel half the apples, leaving the skin on the ones with pink or red color. Core all the apples and chop into roughly 1-inch (2.5-centimeter) pieces.

2   Combine the apples, pear, quince, ¼ cup (60 milliliters) water, the lemon juice, honey, and cinnamon stick in a deep pot over medium heat.

3   Cook until the fruit is broken down and the mixture is thickened, about 40 minutes. Stir frequently, breaking down the fruit by pressing on it and mashing it with a spoon.

4   Serve the applesauce straight from the stove with seared or roasted meat (it's delicious with pork chops), or let cool completely and refrigerate in a clean airtight container.

Makes 2½ cups (600 milliliters)

4 to 6 mixed firm apples (about 3 pounds / 1.4 kilograms), such as Empire or Macoun, some with pink or red skin

1 Anjou or Bartlett pear, peeled, cored, and roughly chopped

1 quince, peeled, cored, and roughly chopped

1 tablespoon freshly squeezed lemon juice (from ½ large lemon)

1 tablespoon honey

1 cinnamon stick

CHILI OIL

Makes 1 cup (240 milliliters)

1 cup (240 milliliters) extra-virgin olive oil

¼ cup (25 grams) red chili flakes

3 cloves garlic, thinly sliced

Of all these stocking-up recipes, I go through this simple hot sauce the fastest. I based it on the chili oil you sometimes see in little glass bottles on the tables in old-style Italian American restaurants. I drizzle it on soup and pizza, add it to store-bought tomato sauce, or just serve it in a dipping bowl with some warm toasted bread.

1   Place all the ingredients in a small saucepan and cook over very low heat for 10 minutes. The heat should be low enough that the garlic sizzles slightly but doesn't fry or change color.

2   Remove from the heat and let cool completely. The garlic and chili flakes will sink to the bottom. Store in the refrigerator and let come to room temperature before using.

A POSTCARD to my grandmother from my sister and me in Hydra, early '80s

GRANOLA

This granola is one of our most popular dishes at The Smile. The trick is to cook it at a low temperature and stir the mixture often so that the oats get evenly crisp and golden. I serve it over Greek yogurt with chopped dried figs and dates, for a hint of North African flavor.

Makes about 10 cups (1 kilogram)

6 cups (480 grams) rolled oats

1½ cups (216 grams) raw almonds, roughly chopped

1½ cups (150 grams) raw pecans, roughly chopped

½ cup (120 milliliters) extra-virgin olive oil

½ cup (120 milliliters) maple syrup

6 tablespoons (110 grams) honey

¼ cup (55 grams) light brown sugar

¼ teaspoon kosher salt

Plain Greek yogurt or milk, for serving

Chopped dried dates, for topping

Chopped dried figs, for topping

Fresh berries, for topping

1   Preheat the oven to 250°F (120°C). Line two baking sheets with parchment paper.

2   In a large bowl, combine the oats, nuts, oil, maple syrup, honey, brown sugar, and salt and mix well.

3   Spread the mixture onto the prepared baking sheets in as even a layer as possible.

4   Bake for 30 minutes, then stir very well. Continue to bake, stirring every 30 minutes, until golden brown and slightly crisp, about 2 hours total.

5   Let cool completely; the oats should feel completely dry and crisp. Transfer to an airtight container and store in a cool, dry place.

6   Serve over Greek yogurt or with milk. Top with dates, figs, and fresh berries.

MARINATED MIXED OLIVES

Makes 1 quart (960 milliliters)

2 cups (360 grams) Alphonso olives

2 cups (360 grams) Greek green olives

Grated zest and juice of 1 orange

4 cloves garlic

2 tablespoons fennel seeds

2 teaspoons red chili flakes

1 cup (240 milliliters) extra-virgin olive oil

I usually have a jar of these olives waiting in the back of my refrigerator for last-minute, low-key entertaining. They make a substantial, flavorful snack to nibble on while enjoying a glass of predinner wine. I like to toss in a few fresh orange slices just before serving.

1 In a heatproof bowl, combine the olives, zest, and juice.

2 Using the side of a chef's knife, lightly press on the garlic cloves so that they crack slightly but stay whole. Add the garlic to the bowl.

3 In a small frying pan over medium-high heat, toast the fennel seeds, stirring constantly, until golden and fragrant but not burnt, about 1 minute.

4 Add the chili flakes and oil to the pan, cook for 30 seconds, then immediately pour the warm oil mixture over the olives and toss to combine.

5 Let cool completely, then transfer to a clean container with a tight-fitting lid (such as a glass canning jar). The olives will keep in the refrigerator for several months.

6 Before serving, let the olives come to room temperature to soften the oil, and mix well with a spoon.

MEYER LEMON CONFIT

At The Smile, we serve a version of this simple condiment on top of our roasted chicken entrée. At home I like to make a batch when Meyer lemons are in season and have it on hand to add a little lemony bite to otherwise simple dishes. It pairs well with roasted chicken, and is great tossed with plain pasta or drizzled over lightly steamed asparagus. For a quick, elegant snack, spread some of the confit on toast and top with torn fresh basil and sea salt. Of course, while Meyer lemons have a particular sweetness, you can also make this recipe using regular lemons.

Makes 1½ cups (360 milliliters)

6 Meyer lemons

1 cup (240 milliliters) extra-virgin olive oil

3 cloves garlic

½ teaspoon kosher salt

1   Use a vegetable peeler to remove the zest of the lemons in strips 2 to 3 inches (5 to 7.5 centimeters) long, leaving as much of the white pith behind as possible. Cut the strips lengthwise into slivers ⅛ inch (3 millimeters) thick.

2   Squeeze ¾ cup (180 milliliters) juice from the lemons (squeeze the remaining juice and reserve for another use, such as in the Ouzo & Meyer Lemon Drops, page 70).

3   Rinse the lemon zest in warm water and drain.

4   In a small saucepan over low heat, combine the zest, juice, oil, garlic, and salt. Bring to a very low simmer and cook until the zest is soft but still holds its shape, about 20 minutes. Skim off and discard the foam that rises to the top of the oil mixture.

5   Let cool completely, then transfer to a clean container with a tight-fitting lid (such as a glass canning jar). Make sure the confit is completely covered with the oil mixture. The confit may be stored in the refrigerator for up to 1 month. Let come to room temperature before using.

MAKERS OF
★ HOMESTEAD ★
HAND DIPPED CANDLES

JUMBO
crevette
396 g)

My*T*Fine
pudding & pie filling
4-1/2 cup servings
NET. WT. 4-1/2 OZ

DAKATINE
PATE D'ARACHIDE

HONIG
custa

CONTENTS   ONE POUND

Peak
COFFE
ROASTED SEE

SCLAFANI
All Natural
MATOES

OURT NATURE
MALO

Attiki

Accent
FLAVOR ENHANCER
ES UP FOOD FLAVO
NET. WT.
osodium Glutamat

Recipe Book Inside 8
junket
RENNET TABLETS
for rennet custard
and ice cream

SERVING
SUGGESTION
NET WT 0.23 OZ
6.5 GRAMS

Spearmint
LEAVES

TANGY
WATERMELON

Spearmint
LEAVES
Lewis

Sip
with your
CIRCUS PALS

COOK AND BE COOL

Sweetheart MOTHER GOO
DRINKING
STRAWS

BORG
SODA

WATE

ARTI

ÔME TORES

ATLAS

CRÉME

PICKLED KUMQUATS

Makes 1 quart (960 milliliters)

4 cups kumquats

1½ cups (360 milliliters) cider vinegar

½ cup (100 grams) sugar

½ teaspoon kosher salt

4 cloves

2 allspice berries

1 bay leaf

½ teaspoon whole black peppercorns

½ teaspoon ground ginger

½ teaspoon ground cinnamon

I love kumquats. I like that you can just throw a whole one in your mouth for a burst of sweet and sour, like nature's candy. Kumquats are usually in stores only for a few months in the winter, so I try to make a batch of these pickles while I can. Serve a little bowl of them alongside a firm goat or sheep's-milk cheese for an instant sophisticated cheese plate.

1   Cut the kumquats in half crosswise and pick out any seeds that are easily accessible.

2   In a saucepan, combine the vinegar, 1 cup (240 milliliters) water, the sugar, salt, and spices and bring to a simmer. Add the kumquats and cook for 1 minute.

3   Transfer to a clean container with a tight-fitting lid (such as a glass canning jar) and let cool completely. Cover and refrigerate. The kumquats will keep in the refrigerator for up to 1 month.

PICKLED RAMPS

Ramps are slender wild leeks that have become extremely trendy in the last few years. Because they can't be cultivated, are hard to transport, and have a short season, they're tailor-made to be fetishized by foodies. I recently overheard a man at the farmers' market scoff that ramps used to be considered a weed and now they're selling for twenty dollars a pound. While I'd love to share his skepticism, I can't help but get on the ramp bandwagon: I have a soft spot for anything in the onion family, and these have an irresistible, delicately sweet yet pungent flavor. They're best sautéed with butter and tossed with orecchiette or spread on toast.

Because their season is so brief, I also like to pickle a bunch while I can get my hands on them (you can sauté the green tops and pickle the rest, as below). Their oniony odor mellows out over time in the sweet pickling mixture. Among my favorite things to make with them are ramp Gibson martinis (page 67). They also make a great simple tomato salad—just finely mince pickled ramps and sprinkle them over sliced ripe beefsteak tomatoes. Drizzle with olive oil and season with salt and pepper.

Makes about 2 cups (480 milliliters)

1 pound (455 grams) ramps

2 limes

2 cups (480 milliliters) distilled white vinegar

½ cup (100 grams) sugar (preferably unrefined cane sugar but conventional sugar will work fine)

¼ cup (73 grams) honey

1 tablespoon whole black peppercorns

2 teaspoons kosher salt

1   Trim the tender, leafy green end of each ramp, leaving about 3 inches (7.5 centimeters) of the white root and stem. Reserve the greens for another use (see headnote).

2   Trim the root end of each ramp. Scrape off any dirt and peel away the outer layer of slimy skin, if present. Rinse well under cold water and set aside.

3   Use a vegetable peeler to remove the zest of the limes in long strips, leaving as much of the white pith behind as possible.

4   In a saucepan, combine the vinegar, 2 cups (480 milliliters) water, the sugar, honey, peppercorns, salt, and zest and bring to a boil.

5   Add the ramps and cook for 1 minute. Remove from the heat.

6   Remove the ramps and place in a clean container with a tight-fitting lid (such as a glass canning jar) and pour the pickling liquid over the ramps until they are well covered. Let cool completely, cover, and refrigerate for at least 3 days before using. The pickles will keep in the refrigerator for several months.

PICKLED RED ONIONS

Makes 1 quart (960 milliliters)

3 medium red onions (about 1½ pounds / 680 grams)

1 cup (240 milliliters) cider vinegar

1 cup (240 milliliters) red wine vinegar

½ cup (110 grams) light brown sugar

2 teaspoons kosher salt

1 fresh Thai chili

1 bay leaf

½ teaspoon mustard seeds

½ teaspoon fennel seeds

½ teaspoon whole black peppercorns

Red onions are intensely flavorful—sweet and pungent, with a crisp, clean texture. Since raw onion, unfortunately, has a lingering aftertaste, I make these pickles to mellow that sharpness while infusing the onions with warm spice notes. You can use them in place of raw onion in salads and on sandwiches.

1   Peel and halve the onions lengthwise. Thinly slice the halves through the root ends into wedges about ¼ inch (6 millimeters) thick and set aside.

2   In a saucepan, combine the remaining ingredients with 1½ cups (360 milliliters) water and bring to a boil. Add the onions. Cook for 1 minute, then remove from the heat. Let cool completely, then transfer to a clean container with a tight-fitting lid (such as a glass canning jar). Cover and refrigerate. The pickles will keep in the refrigerator for up to 2 months.

PINK PICKLES

These are a great snack to have on hand. Soak them the night before you need them, make the pickling mixture in the morning, and let them sit in the fridge until evening. The longer you leave them, the pinker they become. At The Smile, we serve these with all of our sandwiches. The secret to our house salad dressing is that we use the vinegar mixture from these pickles as the base. When you've eaten all the pickles, whisk some of the pickling mixture with a pinch of salt, a squeeze of lemon, and extra-virgin olive oil to make your own delicious salad dressing.

1   *Prepare the vegetables:* Cut the cucumbers into rounds ⅛ inch (3 millimeters) thick (use a mandoline if you have one).

2   Rinse the radishes, discard the green tops, and cut into rounds ⅛ inch (3 millimeters) thick.

3   In a large nonreactive mixing bowl or container, combine 5 cups (1.2 liters) water, the salt, and sugar. Stir well to dissolve. Add the cucumbers and radishes. Cover and let sit overnight. Drain and rinse well with cold water.

4   *Make the pickling mixture:* In a pitcher, combine the vinegar, sugar, garlic, coriander seeds, celery seeds, peppercorns, and ground coriander. Stir to dissolve the sugar.

5   Divide the vegetable mixture and the chilies evenly between two 1-quart (960-milliliter) canning jars (or any other nonreactive containers with tight-fitting lids).

6   Pour the pickling mixture into the jars until the vegetables are completely covered. Cover and refrigerate for at least 5 hours. The pickles will keep in the refrigerator for up to 2 months.

Makes 2 quarts (2 liters)

FOR THE VEGETABLES:

5 Kirby cucumbers

1 bunch radishes (about 6)

1 cup (240 grams) kosher salt

¼ cup (50 grams) sugar

FOR THE PICKLING MIXTURE:

2½ cups (600 milliliters) red wine vinegar

¾ cup (150 grams) sugar

3 cloves garlic, pressed or finely minced

½ teaspoon whole coriander seeds

½ teaspoon celery seeds

½ teaspoon whole pink peppercorns

¼ teaspoon ground coriander

4 fresh habanero chilies

PRESERVED LEMONS

Makes 6

6 lemons, plus more freshly squeezed lemon juice as needed

½ cup (120 grams) kosher salt

2 bay leaves

About ¼ cup (60 milliliters) extra-virgin olive oil

Preserved lemons are essential to Moroccan cooking. They're earthy and salty, with a slightly pickled taste and a mellower acidity than fresh lemons. Add them to braised meats or stews to enrich the flavor, or dice the peel and quickly sauté it with fresh vegetables for a simple but exotic side dish. For a long time I was resistant to making my own, out of sheer impatience—you have to wait for a few weeks for them to be ready—but once we started making them at the restaurant, I realized how easy the process truly is and I felt a little foolish for having bought them for all those years. A little goes a long way, so if you make a batch when you have some extra time (or lemons) on your hands, you'll reap the rewards for months. I've given a bare-bones recipe because I think the lemons hold their own, but feel free to experiment and mix in a few spices at the last stage; a pinch of peppercorns, a few strands of saffron, or a cinnamon stick can be nice additions.

1 Bring a large pot of water to a boil and add the whole lemons; blanch for 2 minutes. Drain and rinse with cold water.

2 Cut each lemon in half crosswise. In a shallow bowl, toss the lemons with the salt until well coated.

3 Press down and cover the lemons with a clean plate and a weight (such as a 28-ounce / 840-millilter can). Let sit at room temperature for a few days to allow the juice to run.

4 Transfer the lemons along with the bay leaves to a clean container with a tight-fitting lid (such as a glass canning jar). Cover with the liquid that the lemons have released. Add more fresh lemon juice until they are completely covered. Drizzle a little olive oil on top, secure the lid, and store at room temperature. The lemons will be ready in 3 weeks. Refrigerate when they are ready and they will keep for several months.

ROSEMARY SALT

I came up with this mixture of fried rosemary and kosher salt when I was experimenting with French fry recipes for the restaurant. I decided a deep fryer was too much of a leap for me, so I ultimately gave up on the fries. Now I sprinkle the salt on potatoes right after they come out of the oven, use it to season a simple roasted chicken, and add it to sandwiches for a punch of flavor.

1   In a small saucepan, heat the oil over medium-high heat for 2 minutes. Drop in a test piece of rosemary to see if the oil is hot enough; it should sizzle on contact.

2   Add the rosemary and cook until it is crisp but still bright green and stops sizzling, about 1 minute. Remove with a slotted spoon and drain on a paper towel.

3   When the rosemary is cool enough to handle, chop it very finely and combine it with the salt. Mix well and transfer to a clean container with a tight-fitting lid. Store in a cool, dry place. The salt will keep for several months.

Makes 1 cup (240 grams)

½ cup (120 milliliters) extra-virgin olive oil

½ cup (20 grams) fresh rosemary leaves, picked from about 1 ounce (30 grams) rosemary sprigs

1 cup (240 grams) kosher salt

SPICED CANDIED PISTACHIOS

Makes 2 cups (300 grams)

1 cup (200 grams) sugar

⅛ teaspoon kosher salt

⅛ teaspoon ground nutmeg

⅛ teaspoon cayenne pepper

2 cups (200 grams) shelled raw pistachios

Nut brittles are a classic candy—the roasty, toffeelike notes in most nuts are a natural match for the burnt sugar. I like using pistachios because they have a pronounced flavor that isn't overwhelmed by the caramel, while the spices lend a bit of depth. I serve these as a sweet snack or easy dessert. Sometimes I roughly chop the brittle and use it to liven up ice cream or store-bought cheesecake. On the savory side, you can sprinkle some over bitter-greens salads to add a sweet-and-spicy note.

1   Lay out a large piece of parchment paper.

2   Place the sugar, salt, nutmeg, and cayenne in a wide heavy-bottomed sauté pan.

3   Cook over medium-high heat, stirring occasionally, until the sugar melts and turns dark golden, about 3 minutes. Be careful—the sugar can burn very quickly. Add the pistachios, remove from the heat, and stir vigorously to coat the nuts in the melted sugar.

4   Pour the mixture onto the parchment paper, spreading it out in one layer. Immediately rinse your sauté pan with warm water so the sugar doesn't harden.

5   Let the brittle cool completely, then break apart into chunks with your hands. Transfer to a clean container with a tight-fitting lid and store in a cool, dry place.

SPICED SUGAR

At The Smile, we serve ruby-red grapefruit halves for breakfast, topped with this lightly spiced sugar. At home I like to have it on hand for throwing together a quick dessert by sprinkling it over fresh berries. Or you can serve the sugar in a bowl alongside some sliced pineapple and mango, squeeze lime juice over the fruit, and dip the fruit into the sugar for a homemade, healthy version of Fun Dip.

In a bowl, combine all the ingredients and mix well. Store in a tightly covered container in a cool, dry place. The sugar will keep indefinitely.

Makes 1 cup (220 grams)

1 cup (220 grams) raw turbinado sugar

½ teaspoon ground cinnamon

½ teaspoon ground ginger

⅛ teaspoon cayenne pepper

⅛ teaspoon ground cardamom

FLOWER ARRANGING

Instead of using vases, arrange fresh flowers in empty food cans of varying sizes. I've heard this advice from a few sources over the years, and it's a technique I always come back to, because I love the way it looks and because I don't own that many real vases. Choose cans with bold colors and attractive designs printed directly onto the metal and clean them well before using. Some of my favorites are Sclafani-brand crushed tomatoes, which have a lovely illustration of a cluster of plum tomatoes on the label, and the imported Greek honey Attiki, which comes in a slender metal canister wrapped in a graphic blue, white, and gold honeycomb pattern. You can also find beautiful vintage coffee cans in all shapes and colors on eBay or at antiques fairs and flea markets. Alternatively, you can soak the label off of any regular can for a clean aluminum look. I like to pair two types of flowers with very different textures, colors, and shapes. For example, combine delicate white chamomile daisies with fuller-blossomed bright orange and pink ranunculus.

I recently bought a vintage cookbook from the 1920s called *Cook and Be Cool.* I couldn't resist the directive in the title. It turned out to be more literal than I thought, referring to "hot weather housekeeping" and summer luncheon recipes that could be made without turning on your oven. The cover is illustrated with a glamorous flapper-style hostess gazing demurely at her elegantly set table, the title in pale pink letters hovering over her head. The collection is presented as a series of formal menus, each one beginning with a carefully conceived appetizer. Reading through it, I could perfectly visualize a single stuffed sardine, tomato canapé, or bouillon wafer sitting placidly in the middle of each plate.

2
APPETIZERS
& DRINKS

Of course, these days most home cooks rarely make anything resembling a traditional appetizer course. Personally, I like to bring all the food out to the table and sit down to eat with my guests, instead of jumping up and running back to the kitchen every five minutes.

The recipes in this chapter aren't for distinct, plated appetizers but rather for casual and delicious snacks that can be nibbled on while waiting for everyone to arrive or to stave off hunger in the kitchen. Set out a bowl of the salty minted snap peas and buy yourself some time to finish cooking. Make any of the dips in advance and place them on the table with a fresh baguette. Encourage everyone to tear off pieces of bread with their hands and enjoy it with the dip all through dinner.

The recipes here are my take on the Greek and Middle Eastern concept of *mezze*, an assortment of small but flavorful dishes to enjoy with a drink before dinner, or that can make up a light meal on their own. This kind of food is perfectly suited for a casual cocktail party. In the summer nothing could be simpler than inviting a few friends over for classic tomato bruschetta (see page 43) and a chilled pitcher of Pink Sangria (page 71). Or take a cue from the forgotten author of *Cook and Be Cool* and go for the elegantly arranged Crudités with Crème Fraîche Dip (page 49).

Most of the drinks in this chapter are designed to pair well with food; the orange flower and almond of the Moroccan Champagne Cocktail (page 66) stand up nicely to the lush figs, creamy ricotta, and assertively fresh basil in the fig crostini (see page 48). While wine always benefits from a bite of fat-rich cheese or a sliver of salami, a cocktail is sometimes best savored on its own. Now that my twenties have officially ended, there's no arguing that I am definitely an adult. It shows my age that recently I've started enjoying a well-made cocktail at home after dinner rather than four or five cheap vodka tonics at a local dive bar. Mixing a good cocktail has some of the same magic as cooking. A martini is the perfect example: A drop of vermouth and a vigorous shake with ice transform gin into something subtly but markedly different. To me, the chill in a cocktail is as essential as heat is to cooking. I've included my two favorite martini recipes here, a variation on a classic Gibson and a cocktail infused with the essential Mediterranean flavors of tomato and caper.

HYDRA PORT in the '70s, when my parents first visited the island

BRUSCHETTA

There's nothing quite like a classic tomato bruschetta to perfectly capture the alchemy of ripe tomatoes, salt, garlic, and basil.

1   Preheat the oven to 400°F (205°C).

2   Bring a pot of water to a boil. Use a sharp knife to make a shallow crisscross on the bottom of each tomato.

3   Set up an ice bath by filling a large bowl with ice and cold water.

4   Place the tomatoes in the boiling water and cook for 30 seconds. Drain the tomatoes and immediately transfer them to the ice bath. When they are cool, use a paring knife to peel the skins off the tomatoes, starting at the corners of your crisscross. Cut the tomatoes in half crosswise; squeeze out and discard the seeds.

5   Dice the tomatoes into roughly ¼-inch (6-millimeter) pieces and combine them with ¼ cup (60 milliliters) of the oil, the salt, garlic, and basil. Set aside at room temperature to allow the flavors to develop.

6   Brush both sides of the bread lightly with the remaining ¼ cup (60 milliliters) oil and place on a baking sheet.

7   Bake until the surface of the bread is toasted and slightly golden but still soft in the center, about 12 minutes.

8   While the bread is still warm, spoon about 6 tablespoons (90 milliliters) of the tomato topping onto each piece, garnish with freshly torn basil, a pinch of salt, and black pepper, if desired. Cut each piece in half on a bias and serve.

Makes 4

6 ripe plum tomatoes (about 1 pound / 455 grams), hulled

½ cup (120 milliliters) extra-virgin olive oil, divided

½ teaspoon kosher salt

2 cloves garlic, pressed or finely minced

5 large basil leaves, thinly sliced, plus more for garnish

4 large slices rustic sourdough bread, cut ¾ inch (2 centimeters) thick

Freshly ground black pepper (optional)

ALMOND DIP

In this easy dip, the slight anise flavor of the dill, the heat of the garlic, and the tanginess of the yogurt somehow work together to bring out the sweetness in the almonds. The fresher the nuts, the better the flavor will be.

1   Place the almonds in a food processor and pulse until they have the texture of bread crumbs, about 30 seconds. If you don't have a food processor, you can go with the DIY method: Place the almonds in a resealable plastic bag and bash them with a rolling pin until you have the right texture.

2   Place the almonds in a bowl and add the remaining ingredients. Stir until well combined and serve with your favorite bread, crackers, or raw vegetables.

3   The dip can be kept refrigerated for several days. To store, cover with plastic wrap pressed directly onto the surface of the dip to prevent it from drying out. Or you can drizzle the top with a thin layer of olive oil (just make sure to let the dip warm up slightly before serving so that the oil comes to room temperature).

Makes 2 to 3 cups (450 to 675 grams)

¼ cup (36 grams) raw whole almonds

1½ cups (375 grams) plain Greek yogurt

⅓ cup (75 milliliters) extra-virgin olive oil, plus more if storing

3 tablespoons (18 grams) finely chopped fresh dill

1 clove garlic, pressed or finely minced

2 tablespoons freshly squeezed lemon juice (from 1 large lemon)

½ teaspoon kosher salt

FAVA BEAN CROSTINI

Serves 4

2½ pounds (1.2 kilograms) fresh fava beans weighed in their pods, shelled (about 2 ½ cups / 300 grams)

10 tablespoons (150 milliliters) extra-virgin olive oil, divided

2 cloves garlic, pressed or finely minced

½ teaspoon kosher salt

Freshly ground black pepper

2 tablespoons roughly chopped fresh parsley

4 large slices rustic sourdough bread, cut ¾ inch (2 centimeters) thick

1 cup (230 grams) fresh ricotta (see page 54)

Flaky sea salt, such as Maldon

This is one of our most popular appetizers at The Smile. I'll admit that working with fresh favas is a bit labor-intensive because you have to shell them twice; however, I like to think that the dense meaty texture and bright, springlike flavor are worth the effort. Peeling the little pods is also great busywork for a friend/spouse/child who wants to help in the kitchen but doesn't want to get involved in anything too heavy-duty.

1   Preheat the oven to 400°F (205°C).

2   Bring a pot of water to a boil. Drop in the fava beans and boil for 2 minutes, then drain and rinse with cold water to stop them from cooking. Peel the pale exterior skin off each bean.

3   Heat 6 tablespoons (90 milliliters) of the oil in a sauté pan over medium heat for 30 seconds. Add the garlic and cook until soft but not browned, 1 to 2 minutes.

4   Add the fava beans and season with the salt and pepper to taste. Cook, stirring often, until the beans are tender but still bright green, 3 to 5 minutes.

5   Remove from the heat, add the parsley, and stir. Let cool.

6   Brush both sides of the bread lightly with the remaining ¼ cup (60 milliliters) oil and place on a baking sheet.

7   Bake until the surface of the bread is toasted and slightly golden but still soft in the center, about 12 minutes.

8   While the bread is still warm, spread ¼ cup (63 grams) ricotta on each piece. Top with about ½ cup (120 milliliters) fava mixture and sprinkle with sea salt. Cut each piece in half on a bias and serve.

FRESH FIG, HONEY & BASIL CROSTINI

Serves 4

4 large slices rustic sourdough bread, cut ¾ inch (2 centimeters) thick

¾ cup (180 milliliters) extra-virgin olive oil

1 cup (250 grams) fresh ricotta (see page 54)

6 ripe fresh figs, at room temperature, stems trimmed, quartered lengthwise

4 large fresh basil leaves

2 teaspoons good-quality honey

Flaky sea salt, such as Maldon, or kosher salt

Freshly ground black pepper

Luxuriously honey-sweet fresh figs have an undeniable sensuality. They're also a rarity, even in this age of year-round imported fruit. In Greece, the trees grow wild in the rocky, sun-drenched environment. The velvety dark purple or green fruits ripen in late July, becoming plump and bursting open to reveal their almost indecently bright magenta insides, attracting a steady, buzzing crowd of hungry bees. In August the uneaten fruit shrivels on the branch, intensifying its sweetness into a dense, candylike morsel.

This crostini is extremely simple but only really works if all the ingredients are at their best—use truly ripe fruit, freshly homemade ricotta, and your favorite honey.

1   Preheat the oven to 400°F (205°C).

2   Place the bread on a baking sheet and brush both sides lightly with the oil.

3   Bake until the bread is toasted and slightly golden on the surface but still soft in the center, about 12 minutes.

4   While the bread is still warm, spread ¼ cup (63 grams) ricotta on each piece. Arrange 6 pieces of fig on each slice, cut side up.

5   Tear the basil leaves into roughly ½-inch (12-millimeter) pieces and scatter them over the figs. Drizzle each slice with ½ teaspoon honey and sprinkle with a pinch of salt and a little pepper.

6   Cut each piece in half on the bias and serve.

CRUDITÉS WITH CRÈME FRAÎCHE DIP

A crudité plate is one of those dishes that can either seem uninspired and depressing or add up to more than the sum of its parts. Raw or lightly cooked vegetables and a simple white dip can look elegant and appetizing. Choose fresh seasonal vegetables, making sure to get a variety of colors, textures, and shapes, and arrange them nicely on a clean platter or cutting board. I'm partial to food that allows you to customize each bite; for this recipe I like to bring a little bowl of celery salt to the table to sprinkle on top of each piece.

1   *Make the dip:* In a bowl, mix all the ingredients together and stir until completely combined.

2   *Make the crudités:* Bring a pot of well-salted water to a boil. Prepare an ice bath by filling a bowl with ice and cold water. Add the sugar snap peas to the boiling water and cook for 30 seconds. Drain the snap peas and immediately transfer to the ice bath until cold. Remove from the ice bath and set aside.

3   Trim the root end of the fennel, halve lengthwise, and discard the tough outer layer. Cut out and discard the white core, leaving enough so that the pieces hold together. Cut lengthwise into wedges ¼ inch (6 millimeters) thick.

4   Quarter the radishes lengthwise.

5   Arrange all the vegetables loosely on a platter. I like to form a pile and sprinkle the radishes on top. Serve with the dip and a small bowl of celery salt.

Makes about 1½ cups (335 grams)

FOR THE DIP:

1 cup (250 grams) crème fraîche

½ cup (120 milliliters) buttermilk

2 teaspoons freshly squeezed lemon juice (from ½ small lemon)

1 tablespoon finely chopped fresh dill

¼ teaspoon kosher salt

¼ teaspoon sugar

Pinch of cayenne pepper

FOR THE CRUDITÉS:

1 cup (125 grams) raw sugar snap peas, strings removed

1 fennel bulb, top removed, washed

1 small bunch radishes, green tops removed, washed

1 bunch whole baby carrots (not the bagged supermarket kind), tops removed, washed

Celery salt

THROW-IT-IN-THE-OVEN GARLIC BREAD

Makes 8 pieces

¼ cup (60 milliliters) extra-virgin olive oil

6 cloves garlic

1 white French baguette

2 tablespoons unsalted butter, softened

1 teaspoon dried oregano

In my version of this red-sauce restaurant staple, I use garlic oil so you get that intense flavor without eating a huge mouthful of pure garlic.

1   Preheat the oven to 425°F (220°C).

2   Place the oil in a small bowl. Using a garlic press, crush all the cloves directly into the oil (so the oil catches all the garlic juice). Stir and let stand for at least 15 minutes.

3   Pour the oil through a fine-mesh strainer into another bowl; using the back of a spoon, press on the garlic in the strainer to release more juices into the oil. Discard the garlic solids.

4   Slice the baguette in half lengthwise and place both halves, cut side up, on a baking sheet. Spread 1 tablespoon butter on each half. Drizzle with the garlic oil and sprinkle with the oregano.

5   Bake until slightly golden and toasty, about 10 minutes.

6   Cut each half into 4 pieces and serve warm.

MANCHEGO & SUNGOLD-TOMATO-JAM SANDWICHES

Grilled cheese is one of the most satisfyingly basic comfort foods. Here I've added the influence of Spanish ingredients to the rich and buttery all-American classic. The Manchego has a delicate nutty flavor that blends nicely with the intensely fruity Sungold tomatoes and the bite of the pickled onion. I serve these for lunch with a bowl of Roasted-Tomato Soup (page 97), but they're also a big hit as a cocktail-party snack.

1   *Make the jam:* In a wide saucepan over medium-high heat, combine all the ingredients plus 2 tablespoons water and bring to a simmer. Cook, stirring occasionally, until the mixture is completely broken down, reduced, and thickened, 20 to 30 minutes. It should have a sticky, jamlike texture. Set aside. (The jam may also be covered and refrigerated for up to 1 month.)

2   Preheat the oven to 400°F (205°C).

3   *Make the sandwiches:* For one sandwich, spread about 1½ tablespoons of tomato jam on both slices of bread. Sprinkle ½ cup (50 grams) of cheese on one slice. Top with about 8 pieces of pickled onion, and place the other slice on top. Repeat for the remaining 3 sandwiches.

4   In a frying pan, heat 2 tablespoons (30 grams) of the butter over medium-high heat until melted and bubbling. Place 2 sandwiches in the pan and cook, pressing down on the bread with a spatula, until the bread is slightly golden, 1 to 2 minutes. Flip and repeat on the other side.

5   Place the sandwiches on a baking sheet. Wipe the frying pan with a paper towel. Heat the remaining 2 tablespoons (30 grams) butter and brown the remaining 2 sandwiches; transfer them to the baking sheet. (If you're making these for a cocktail party, you can hold them at this stage, slice them into 3 pieces each, and reheat in the oven right before serving.)

6   Place the baking sheet in the oven and cook until the cheese is completely melted, about 5 minutes. Cut each sandwich in half and serve both halves for a full serving.

Makes 4 full or 12 appetizer-size sandwiches

FOR THE JAM:

2 pints (600 grams) Sungold tomatoes, halved

2 tablespoons sugar

2 tablespoons cider vinegar

¼ teaspoon kosher salt

Pinch of ground coriander

Pinch of cayenne pepper

FOR THE SANDWICHES:

8 slices rustic sourdough bread cut ¾ inch (2 centimeters) thick

4 ounces (115 grams) young Manchego cheese, rind removed, grated (about 2 cups)

Pickled red onions (see page 34), about 32 pieces

4 tablespoons (50 grams) unsalted butter, divided

MARINATED GOAT CHEESE

with Fried Garlic & Sage

When I plate this dish at The Smile, I always think that the combination of snow-white goat cheese, dark green sage, and pink peppercorns looks like Christmas. You can serve the cheese as soon as it's ready or you can store it in the fridge for later; the extra time soaking with the garlicky oil will intensify the flavor, but the sage and garlic won't be as crisp. Make sure to let the cheese and oil come to room temperature before serving—with lots of bread.

Serves 4 to 6 as a hearty appetizer or snack

3 cloves garlic

10 tablespoons (150 milliliters) extra-virgin olive oil, divided

6 fresh sage leaves

2 teaspoons herbes de Provence

2 teaspoons pink peppercorns (see Note)

8 ounces (225 grams) soft goat cheese in a log (usually about ½ log), very cold

1   Slice the garlic lengthwise as thinly as possible; it should be almost translucent (use a mandoline if you have one).

2   Place 2 tablespoons (30 milliliters) of the oil in a heatproof container and set aside.

3   In a small saucepan, heat the remaining ½ cup (120 milliliters) oil over medium-high heat for 2 minutes. Drop in a test piece of garlic to see if the oil is hot enough; it should sizzle on contact.

4   Add the garlic and cook for 20 seconds, stirring to make sure all the slices are separated. Add the sage and cook until the garlic is just slightly golden and has stopped sizzling, about 40 more seconds. Remove from the heat.

5   Add the herbes de Provence and pink peppercorns, then immediately pour the hot oil mixture into the bowl of cold oil to stop the garlic from cooking. Let cool.

6   Using a piece of string or plain dental floss, cut the goat cheese into four rounds, each ¾ inch (2 centimeters) thick. Place the rounds on a serving dish. Arrange some of the fried garlic and sage on top of each piece of cheese and drizzle most of the oil over everything. Serve.

NOTE: Pink peppercorns are young, tender peppercorns that are much softer and have a sweeter flavor than regular black peppercorns.

RICOTTA

Makes about 1¾ cups (440 grams)

2 quarts (2 liters) good-quality
  whole milk

1 cup (240 milliliters) heavy cream

1 cup (240 milliliters) buttermilk

2 tablespoons freshly squeezed lemon
  juice (from 1 large lemon)

½ teaspoon kosher salt, or more
  to taste

⅛ teaspoon ground white pepper

So often the labor-intensive home version of a basic ingredient isn't worth the effort, especially when there are so many options made by experts at your fingertips. I always thought that homemade ricotta was one of those things—far too much of a pain to possibly be worth it. Then, of course, when I actually tried making it, I realized it's incredibly simple and tastes infinitely better than the grocery-store version. I use a mixture of whole milk and heavy cream for a smoother, more spreadable texture.

1   In a large pot, combine the milk, cream, buttermilk, lemon juice, and salt and stir once.

2   Cook, without stirring, over medium heat until the mixture appears curdled and separated, about 20 minutes, then remove from the heat. Make sure the mixture never reaches more than a gentle simmer or the curds will break up and become tough. If it starts to boil, turn the heat to medium-low.

3   Fit a fine-mesh strainer over a large bowl. Use a slotted spoon to ladle all the separated cheese curd from the mixture into the strainer.

4   Let sit until most of the liquid has drained out and the ricotta is firm, at least 10 minutes. Discard the liquid in the cooking pot.

5   Transfer the drained curd to a separate bowl and save the liquid that has drained into the first mixing bowl. Add the white pepper to the curd and stir well, then season with more salt to taste, if desired. If the ricotta seems too dry, stir in a little of the reserved liquid until you have a good consistency. It should be creamy and spreadable but not watery.

6   I love to eat it while it's still warm, but the ricotta can be stored, covered, in the refrigerator for up to 1 week.

ROASTED-CARROT DIP

For this recipe I roast chopped carrots with whole coriander and cumin seeds before blending them with feta and honey. The roasting brings out the sweetness of the carrots while lightly toasting the whole spices, giving them a richer, nuttier flavor. The preserved lemon adds a salty, intensified citrus note to an unexpected dip.

Serve with warmed pita bread, sliced baguette, your favorite crackers, or freshly cut vegetables.

1   Preheat the oven to 400°F (205°C).

2   In a bowl, toss together the carrots, preserved lemon, 2 tablespoons (30 milliliters) of the oil, the coriander, cumin, ¼ teaspoon of the salt, and pepper to taste. Spread the mixture on a baking sheet in a single layer. Roast until the carrots are tender and browned at the edges, about 30 minutes. Let cool.

3   Place the carrots, honey, cheese, the remaining ¼ teaspoon salt, and the remaining 3 tablespoons (45 milliliters) oil in a blender or food processor and blend on high speed until smooth. Serve, or cover and refrigerate for up to 1 week.

Makes 2 cups (450 grams)

4 large carrots (about 1 pound / 455 grams), scrubbed and cut into ½-inch (1.5-centimeter) thick rounds

½ preserved lemon (see page 36), seeds removed, roughly chopped

5 tablespoons (75 milliliters) extra-virgin olive oil, divided

1 tablespoon whole coriander seeds

2 teaspoons whole cumin seeds

½ teaspoon kosher salt, divided

Freshly ground black pepper

1 teaspoon honey

¾ cup (90 grams) crumbled feta cheese

MINTED SNAP PEAS

Serves 4

FOR THE MINT OIL:

½ cup (120 milliliters) extra-virgin olive oil

8 fresh mint sprigs (about ½ small bunch)

FOR THE PEAS:

2 tablespoons (30 grams) kosher salt

1 pound (455 grams) sugar snap peas, strings removed

1 tablespoon plus 1 teaspoon finely chopped fresh mint

½ teaspoon flaky sea salt, such as Maldon

Mint and peas are one of the world's great flavor combinations, instantly evoking the fresh green aroma of spring. Local seasonal sugar snaps, with their full natural sweetness, are the best, but good-quality supermarket snap peas are still delicious. Look for bright green color and plump pods.

The magic here is that the oil coats the snap peas with a more intense minty flavor than fresh herbs would impart on their own. I like to serve these in chilled bowls as finger food, a healthy vegetable alternative to salty bar snacks that you can put out at parties instead of chips or pretzels. You can also serve them in one big bowl as a cold side dish, a good option for family-style dinners, picnics, or barbecues.

1   *Make the mint oil:* In a small saucepan, heat the oil over high heat until very hot, about 2 minutes. Test the temperature by dropping in a mint leaf; if the oil is hot enough, the leaf will sizzle on contact. Drop the mint sprigs (stems included) into the oil, cook for 30 seconds, then remove the saucepan from the heat. The mint should sizzle, fry, and become crisp but not burnt. Let cool completely, then fish out and discard the mint.

2   *Make the peas:* Bring a large pot of water and the kosher salt to a boil. Set up an ice bath by filling a bowl with ice and cold water. Add the snap peas to the boiling water and cook for 30 seconds. It's very important not to overcook the snap peas; you want them to lose that raw taste but still be bright green and crisp. Drain and transfer to the ice bath immediately.

3   Drain the snap peas and divide them among four small chilled bowls. Drizzle with about 1 tablespoon mint oil per bowl. Sprinkle with the fresh mint and sea salt and serve.

GREEK FAVA: YELLOW SPLIT PEA PUREE

Makes 2 to 3 cups (480 to 720 milliliters); serves 4 as a side dish

1 cup (330 grams) dried yellow split peas, picked over to remove any rocks, rinsed

1 bay leaf

1¼ teaspoons kosher salt, divided

½ cup (120 milliliters) extra-virgin olive oil, plus more for drizzling

1 clove garlic, pressed or finely minced

1 small shallot, peeled and roughly chopped

1 tablespoon freshly squeezed lemon juice (from ½ large lemon)

1 tablespoon red wine vinegar

4 kalamata olives

¼ red onion, cut into ¼-inch (6-millimeter) dice (optional)

½ lemon, cut into wedges (optional)

In Greece this dip is simply called *fava,* confusing English speakers because it has nothing to do with what we call fava beans. It's one of those dishes that is actually very simple but every taverna, in Greece as well as in Greek neighborhoods around the world, has its own slightly different take. I tend to use the quality of the fava as a litmus test when choosing my favorite Greek restaurants. Here, I tried to mimic the traits I like most—a creamy texture, full but not overpowering onion flavor, and a bit of acidic kick from the vinegar. It can be served warm or cold, and can be eaten as a starter, a side dish, or a snack (like hummus).

1   In a medium-size pot, combine the split peas with 5 cups (1.2 liters) water, the bay leaf, and 1 teaspoon of the salt and bring to a boil. Reduce the heat to a simmer and cook until the split peas are completely soft, about 30 minutes.

2   Drain well, remove and discard the bay leaf, and let cool slightly. Most of the water will have been absorbed by the split peas.

3   In a blender or food processor, combine the split peas with the oil, garlic, shallot, lemon juice, vinegar, and the remaining ½ teaspoon salt and blend on high speed until creamy and smooth, 1 to 2 minutes.

4   Transfer to a small serving bowl or plate, drizzle with oil, sprinkle with the olives and onion, if desired, and serve with lemon wedges, if desired.

TZATZIKI

No Mediterranean cookbook would be complete without a recipe for *tzatziki*. I based this recipe on the version served at Aliada, a small restaurant in Astoria, Queens: I use lots of cucumber and thick yogurt, and give it a pronounced garlic undertone. *Tzatziki* is a great addition to fried or grilled vegetables, especially zucchini. Of course it also can be eaten by itself, with lots of warm fresh bread.

1 Peel the cucumbers completely, cut them in half lengthwise, and scoop out and discard the seeds.

2 Grate the cucumbers using the medium-size holes of a box grater, or in a food processor using the shredding attachment.

3 Place the grated cucumber in a fine-mesh strainer fitted over a bowl. Sprinkle with the 1 teaspoon salt and let sit 15 minutes to draw the moisture out of the cucumbers so they won't make the dip soggy.

4 Wrap the cucumbers in a clean kitchen towel or paper towel and press to remove excess moisture.

5 In a medium-size serving bowl, combine the cucumbers with the remaining ingredients and mix well. Taste for seasoning and add more salt if desired. Clean the sides of the bowl with a paper towel and serve.

Makes 2½ cups (625 grams)

2 cucumbers (about 1½ pounds / 680 grams)

1 teaspoon kosher salt, or more to taste

2 cups (500 grams) full-fat plain Greek yogurt

2 tablespoons extra-virgin olive oil

2 tablespoons finely chopped fresh dill

2 cloves garlic, pressed or finely minced

1½ tablespoons freshly squeezed lemon juice (from ¾ large lemon)

INDIAN QUEEN HOTEL
The Pride of Stroudsburg

ROOM WINE LIST

FRITTATA

Serves 4 to 6

10 large eggs

2 tablespoons whole milk

¾ teaspoon kosher salt, divided

3 tablespoons (45 milliliters) extra-virgin olive oil

½ yellow onion, thinly sliced

1 red bell pepper, halved lengthwise, seeded, and thinly sliced crosswise

4 ounces (115 grams) spicy pork sausage meat, removed from casing

I used to be biased against frittatas, based on years of bad diner renditions that resembled stiff, overcooked omelets. Done right, a frittata is fluffy, flavorful, and incredibly easy to make for a quick brunch. Unlike most egg dishes, a frittata is traditionally served at room temperature; you can cook it in advance, toss together a simple salad, and have a lovely low-key meal. The only trick is to use a well-seasoned (preferably cast-iron) frying pan so the eggs won't stick to the bottom.

1   Preheat the oven to 400°F (205°C).

2   In a bowl, combine the eggs, milk, and ½ teaspoon of the salt and whisk vigorously until completely blended.

3   In a well-seasoned 10-inch (25-centimeter) ovenproof (preferably cast-iron) frying pan, heat the oil over medium-high heat for 30 seconds. Add the onion, pepper, and the remaining ¼ teaspoon salt. Cook, stirring often, until the onion is soft and translucent, about 4 minutes.

4   Add the sausage and cook, breaking it up with a spoon, until completely cooked through, 2 to 3 minutes.

5   Add the egg mixture. Stir gently with a wooden spoon, scraping the sides and bottom of the pan as you would with scrambled eggs. Cook until the eggs are just beginning to set, about 2 minutes.

6   Transfer the pan to the oven and cook until the frittata is puffed up and firm, about 10 minutes.

7   Let cool slightly. The frittata will deflate and the edges will shrink away from the sides of the pan. I like to bring the whole thing to the table and slice it into wedges directly in the pan. Use a spatula to lift out each piece and serve.

LIME SHANDIES

My mom always used to order a Sprite and a Greek beer at the cafés in the port on Hydra. She would mix them in a glass bit by bit, while shooing away the yellow jackets that would land on the rims of the bottles. I make this homemade lime syrup for the same effect—without watering down the beer as much.

1   *Make the lime syrup:* In a small saucepan, combine the lime juice and sugar and cook over medium heat until the sugar is completely dissolved, about 2 minutes. Remove from the heat, let cool completely, cover, and refrigerate. (The syrup will keep, refrigerated, for up to 1 month.)

2   *To make 1 shandy:* Place the lime syrup in a tall glass and fill the glass with beer, or add the lime shandy directly into the bottle of your favorite medium-bodied beer. Garnish with the lime wedge.

Makes 6

FOR ¾ CUP (180 MILLILITERS) LIME SYRUP:

½ cup (120 milliliters) freshly squeezed lime juice (from about 4 limes)

½ cup (100 grams) sugar

FOR EACH SHANDY:

1 bottle medium-bodied beer

2 tablespoons lime syrup

1 lime wedge

HIBISCUS ICED TEA

In bloom, hibiscus flowers are audaciously vibrant, the bright explosion of red reproduced on so many Hawaiian shirts. Dried, they have an intensely earthy flavor, a tannic texture, and a dark blood-red color. This makes them ideal ingredients for a richly flavored iced tea, which happens to look beautiful in a glass pitcher when the sun is shining through it. Of course, if you prefer, you can also drink the tea hot or spiked with your alcohol of choice.

1   In a saucepan over medium-high heat, combine the hibiscus, cinnamon stick, allspice, orange zest, ginger, and sugar with 4 cups (960 milliliters) water. Bring to a simmer and cook for 1 minute. Remove from the heat and let infuse in the pot until cooled completely. Taste for sweetness and add more sugar, if desired.

2   Strain into a pitcher and refrigerate until cold. Discard the solids.

3   Serve over ice, garnished with an orange half round, if desired.

Makes 4 cups (960 milliliters)

1 cup (40 grams) dried hibiscus flowers

1 cinnamon stick

3 allspice berries

1 strip orange zest

1 (1-inch / 2.5-centimeter) piece fresh ginger, peeled and cut into strips

¼ cup (50 grams) sugar, or more to taste

1 orange, cut into half rounds ¼ inch (6 millimeters) thick (optional)

MOROCCAN CHAMPAGNE COCKTAIL

Makes 1

1 raw cane sugar cube

⅛ teaspoon orange-flower water

Very cold sparkling wine

1 teaspoon amaretto liqueur, such as Disaronno

1 strip orange zest, 2 inches (5 centimeters) long and 1 inch (2.5 centimeters) wide (see Note)

I'm a sucker for a classic champagne cocktail. The simple elegance of sparkling wine dressed up with a sugar cube, a drop of bitters, and a lemon twist evokes visions of another era full of glamorous women in black cocktail dresses and diamonds slinking through dimly lit hotel bars. My version is inspired by what I consider to be the quintessential Moroccan flavor combination: orange and almond.

1   Place the sugar cube in a champagne glass and add the orange-flower water.

2   Fill the glass with sparkling wine and add the amaretto.

3   Hold the orange zest over the mouth of the glass with both hands and twist lightly to release the oil in the skin; drop the zest into the cocktail and serve.

NOTE: Use a vegetable peeler or sharp paring knife to remove the skin of the orange without getting any of the white pith.

PICKLED-RAMP GIBSON

After extensive—and enjoyable—research, I've come to the conclusion that I like my martinis very cold and very dry. To that end, I use very little vermouth, keep my gin in the freezer, and shake with ice to get that thin, barely frozen layer on top of the cocktail. Naturally, you can adjust the recipe according to your own martini preferences. This update on the classic Gibson, a variation made with cocktail onions, was inspired by a drink I had the first time I went to the restaurant Blue Hill at Stone Barns. The idea of onions and alcohol may be off-putting to some, but for me the sweet, pungent, and slight citrusy tang from the pickle juice is a perfect, subtle complement to the gin. My favorite part is gobbling up the alcohol-soaked ramp at the end.

1   Fill a cocktail shaker with ice and add the gin, vermouth, and pickling liquid.

2   Shake vigorously for 20 seconds, then strain into a chilled martini glass.

3   Garnish with the pickled ramp.

Makes 1

2 ounces (60 milliliters) very cold gin

½ teaspoon dry vermouth

½ teaspoon pickling liquid from pickled ramps (see page 33)

1 pickled ramp (see page 33)

TOMATO-WATER & CAPER-BERRY MARTINI

Makes 4

FOR 1 CUP (240 MILLILITERS)
TOMATO WATER (ENOUGH FOR
4 MARTINIS):

1 pound (455 grams) ripe vine
tomatoes

1 tablespoon freshly squeezed lemon
juice (from ½ large lemon)

1 teaspoon celery salt

4 fresh basil leaves, torn

FOR EACH MARTINI:

¼ cup (60 milliliters) tomato water

2 ounces (60 milliliters) very cold gin
(or vodka, if you prefer)

½ teaspoon dry vermouth

½ teaspoon brine from the
caper-berry jar

1 caper berry

Black pepper

The caper berry is the fruit of a wild crawling vine that grows all over the Mediterranean and is the source of an essential ingredient in any Mediterranean kitchen. Capers as we know them are the plucked and cured buds of caper flowers; if left untouched, the buds bloom into bursts of delicate white petals surrounding a shock of dark purple stamens.

Pickled caper berries are available in most good grocery stores and are denser and meatier than the much smaller capers. Here, they're the perfect salty complement to the tomato water and a nice visual substitute for the classic olive garnish. This cocktail is a bit like a Bloody Mary pared down to its essential flavors: tomato, lemon, a dash of celery salt, and a bit of spice from the black pepper.

1   *Make the tomato water:* Roughly chop the tomatoes and place them in a bowl. Add the remaining ingredients and let sit at room temperature for at least 10 minutes. Transfer the mixture to a fine-mesh strainer fitted over a bowl. Using the back of a spoon, press the liquid out of the tomatoes until you have 1 cup juice. Discard the solids.

2   *To make 1 martini:* Fill a cocktail shaker with ice and add the tomato water, gin, vermouth, and brine. Shake vigorously for 20 seconds, then strain into a chilled martini glass.

3   Pierce the caper berry with a cocktail skewer and drop it into the glass. Finely grind some black pepper on top and serve.

OUZO & MEYER LEMON DROPS

Makes 4

⅓ cup (75 milliliters) freshly squeezed Meyer lemon juice (from 2 large Meyer lemons)

1 tablespoon sugar

2.5 ounces (75 milliliters) ouzo

I came up with this drink to use up the Meyer lemon juice left over from a batch of lemon confit (see page 29). This takes me back to my teenage years in Greece in the 1990s, when I used to do shots at the now closed Disco Heaven in Hydra (yes, they were still called discos then). Ouzo is a bit of an acquired taste, but I find that the sweet lemon offsets the pronounced anise flavor in a nice way.

1   In a cocktail shaker, combine the lemon juice and sugar and stir to dissolve.

2   Fill the shaker with ice and add the ouzo. Cover and shake vigorously for 20 seconds.

3   Pour into four shot glasses and drink immediately.

PINK SANGRIA

In the summertime at The Smile, we serve pitchers of this sangria and can barely keep up with the demand. The rosé is lighter bodied than a red wine and blends well with the fruit juices, while imparting an appealing rosy-pink color. I've suggested some fruit, but use whatever you find that looks appetizing and ripe.

1 In a large pitcher, combine the wine, juices, and sugar and stir to dissolve.

2 Cut the plum, nectarine, and orange into half rounds ¼ inch (6 millimeters) thick. Add all the fruit to the pitcher.

3 Pour into ice-filled glasses and serve.

Makes about 8 servings

1 (750-milliliter) bottle dry rosé wine

2 cups (480 milliliters) ruby-red grapefruit juice

1 cup (240 milliliters) orange juice

¼ cup (50 grams) sugar

1 red plum, halved and pitted

1 nectarine, halved and pitted

1 orange, halved

1 cup (155 grams) cherries, pitted

Almost everything I cook is best served family style, heaped in a bowl or on a platter. I've never been interested in making the kind of food that involves arranging each element of the dish in a delicately balanced tower on the plate. I'd rather eat a simply presented home-cooked meal than a composed imitation of a four-star-restaurant dish. However, that's not to say that I don't value the aesthetic quality of my food; just because a dish is simple, it doesn't mean it can't be beautiful. I find that when you focus on the naturally striking qualities in your ingredients, it's easy to create an effortlessly attractive meal.

3

SALADS

Matt, the co-owner of The Smile, always jokes that I should write a cookbook called "cooking with color" because of my preoccupation with brightly colored produce. More than any other dish, salads are perfect vehicles for displaying the amazing variations that you find in fresh raw fruit and vegetables. Reading over my recipes, I notice the consistent repetition of visual references; I find myself constantly calling attention to contrasting colors and layering textures. To me, enjoying a great meal encompasses more than just consuming food. The ritual of eating includes a full range of experiences: the allure of the initial visual presentation, the appetite-arousing mingled aromas, and the satisfaction of that first taste. I love the way a single dash of color looks against the pale greens of a bed of lettuce—the bright magentas of radishes or the deep golds and purples of sliced plums. The raw elements of the salads seem to project their flavors more readily than their cooked counterparts. The deep green of finely shredded kale hints at its complex mineral-like flavor, while the bubblegum pink of watermelon proclaims its juicy sweetness.

Perhaps because of this directness, salads are among my favorite things to make and to eat. I like the casual feeling of tossing together a few select elements of flavor and texture. Because salads are simple and don't involve anything technically impressive (no pyrotechnics or foams here), they can often be afterthoughts on a restaurant menu, and I'm always pleasantly surprised when I eat out and have a truly delicious or inventive salad. For me, the trick is to not go overboard on the ingredients, which can lead to overwrought concoctions with dissonant flavors. There's a loose formula I like to follow: a bit of crunch, a hint of sweetness, a pinch of salt, and once in a while one rich, creamy, fatty ingredient that brings the others into sharp focus. When I'm at home during the day I like to root through my fridge and pull together a simple salad for lunch. The limitations can be inspiring, forcing me to follow my taste buds and create something out of very little. The raw winter salad I've included here came out of a fridge full of forgotten root vegetables I had meant to use in a soup.

I was raised eating salad European style, at the end of every meal. I have no idea why my parents did it that way but, as with so many arbitrary childhood patterns, it stuck. I like how it gives me something to look forward to during the meal, while making for a light and crisp palate cleanser. I often have that thought in mind when cooking at home—in my take on a classic Greek lettuce salad, the acidity of the lemon and freshness of the dill perfectly balance a heavy or particularly rich dinner. For the dressing recipes, I've erred on the side of having a bit extra rather than too little. Drizzle your dressing slowly and hold back if you prefer your salad more lightly dressed. Toss gently but thoroughly to make sure all the elements are evenly coated. While I've created each dressing specifically for the combination of flavors in its salad, feel free to mix and match if it feels right to you.

Another BOAT PICNIC (mid-'90s)

ARUGULA SALAD

with Roasted Grape Tomatoes

Here, the sweetness of the roasted tomatoes balances out the distinct peppery spiciness of the arugula. I use the tomato-infused oil from the roasting pan as the base of the dressing to get even more of that rich, roasted flavor into the salad. The warm tomatoes will slightly wilt some of the arugula, a rustic look that brings the salad together. This goes very well with egg dishes for a delicious, simple brunch.

Serves 4

1 pint (300 grams) red grape tomatoes

5 tablespoons (75 milliliters) extra-virgin olive oil, divided

½ teaspoon kosher salt, divided

Freshly ground black pepper

1 tablespoon white wine vinegar

½ teaspoon sugar

6 cups wild arugula (about 4 ounces / 115 grams)

1 Preheat the oven to 400°F (205°C).

2 On a baking sheet or in a roasting pan, toss the tomatoes with 2 tablespoons (30 milliliters) of the oil, ¼ teaspoon of the salt, and pepper to taste. Roast until most of the tomatoes have burst open slightly and are browned around the edges, about 25 minutes.

3 Pour off the oil and juice from the baking sheet into a small bowl or cup to use as the base of the dressing. Add the vinegar, sugar, and the remaining ¼ teaspoon salt. Mix with a fork to combine. Add the remaining 3 tablespoons (45 milliliters) oil and whisk with a fork until emulsified.

4 Let the tomatoes cool slightly, then toss most of them with the arugula. Drizzle with dressing and toss to coat. Top with the reserved tomatoes and serve.

BEET & WATERMELON-RADISH SALAD

with Buffalo Mozzarella

Serves 4

FOR THE CITRUS DRESSING:

1 tablespoon freshly squeezed orange juice (from ¼ orange)

1 tablespoon freshly squeezed lemon juice (from ½ large lemon)

¼ teaspoon kosher salt

¼ cup (60 milliliters) extra-virgin olive oil

FOR THE SALAD:

3 medium red beets (about 1 pound / 455 grams), with tops and greens removed

½ medium orange, cut into 4 pieces

A few fresh thyme sprigs

1 teaspoon kosher salt

3 tablespoons (45 milliliters) extra-virgin olive oil

1 large watermelon radish (or 4 medium red radishes), cut into very thin rounds (see Note)

8 ounces (225 grams) buffalo mozzarella

4 large fresh basil leaves

Sea salt

Freshly ground black pepper

My mother's close friend, an Italian woman, once discovered beets and mozzarella being served at one of Mario Batali's restaurants and adamantly insisted that it was a strange and unallowable combination, too much of a deviation from the classic cooking she grew up with on the Amalfi coast. To me, there is a natural affinity between the earthy beets and creamy mozzarella both in texture and flavor, the fresh milky cheese melting into the dense root vegetable with each bite, offset by the pleasantly bright citrus dressing and burst of freshly torn basil.

1   *Make the citrus dressing:* In a small bowl or cup, combine the juices and salt and stir well to dissolve. Add the oil and whisk with a fork until emulsified.

2   *Make the salad:* Preheat the oven to 400°F (205°C).

3   Rinse the beets well and place them in a baking dish. Arrange the orange pieces around the beets. Top with the thyme sprigs, then sprinkle with the kosher salt and drizzle with the oil.

4   Pour 1 cup (240 milliliters) water over the beets and cover the dish with aluminum foil. Poke a few holes in the foil and roast the beets until completely tender, 45 minutes to 1 hour.

5   Uncover the beets, and as soon as they are cool enough to handle, use a cloth or paper towel to rub off the beet skins. Halve the beets lengthwise and cut each half into 5 wedges.

6   Arrange the radish slices in an overlapping single layer on a plate or platter. Top with the beet wedges. Tear the mozzarella into 1-inch (2.5-centimeter) pieces with your hands and sprinkle over the beets.

7   Tear the basil into pieces and sprinkle over the salad. Drizzle with the dressing, season to taste with sea salt and pepper, and serve.

NOTE: A watermelon radish is a large radish with a pale green exterior and bright magenta interior. It's available in some supermarkets and farmers' markets.

BUTTERHEAD LETTUCE & RADISH SALAD

Serves 4 to 6

FOR THE DRESSING:

2 tablespoons red wine vinegar

1 teaspoon freshly squeezed lemon juice (from ¼ small lemon)

¾ teaspoon sugar

½ teaspoon kosher salt

¼ teaspoon celery seeds

¼ cup (60 milliliters) extra-virgin olive oil

FOR THE SALAD:

2 heads butterhead (also known as Bibb or Boston) lettuce (about 1 pound / 455 grams)

4 red radishes

I think it's important to have an extremely simple leafy salad in your arsenal, something light and refreshing to serve with a heavy meal like a seared steak or a big meaty roast. I love the way whole butterhead lettuce leaves look piled high on top of each other, the tender pale green dotted with bright magenta radishes. This dressing is the one I make most often at home, a very basic vinaigrette punched up with subtly aromatic celery seeds.

1   *Make the dressing:* In a small bowl or cup, combine the vinegar, lemon juice, sugar, salt, and celery seeds and mix well to dissolve the sugar and salt. Add the oil and whisk with a fork until emulsified.

2   *Make the salad:* Cut off and discard the root end of the lettuce and gently detach the leaves, keeping them whole. Discard any brown or wilted leaves. Rinse gently with cold water and dry in a salad spinner. Arrange the lettuce leaves in a large serving bowl.

3   Trim off the ends of the radishes and cut them into very thin rounds. Add most of the radishes to the serving bowl, holding back a few to scatter on top for garnish.

4   Drizzle with most of the dressing and toss well to combine. Top with the reserved radishes, add the last bit of dressing, and serve.

FENNEL, CUCUMBER & POMEGRANATE SALAD

A refreshing mix of crunchy, sweet, salty, and fresh herb flavors, strewn with jewel-like pomegranate seeds, this is one of my favorite salads to serve with a buffet-style meal. It's beautiful and substantial, a lovely addition to any feast.

1   *Make the dressing:* In a small bowl or cup, combine the vinegar, salt, and sugar and mix well to dissolve. Add the oil and whisk with a fork until emulsified.

2   *Make the salad:* Trim off the root ends and tops of the fennel, reserving some of the tender green fronds. Cut each bulb in half lengthwise and remove the tough outer layers and dense white core. Slice as thinly as possible lengthwise and place in a large serving bowl.

3   Peel the cucumber, cut it in half lengthwise, and scoop out the seeds with a spoon; discard the seeds. Cut into half rounds ¼ inch (6 millimeters) thick and add to the bowl.

4   Add the cilantro, parsley, mint, and the reserved fennel fronds.

5   Cut the pomegranate in half and reserve one half for another use. Hold the fruit over a separate bowl and hit it with the back of a wooden spoon to knock the seeds out. Pick out any bits of white membrane that stick to the seeds. You should have about ½ cup (60 grams) seeds.

6   Just before serving, add the feta and most of the pomegranate seeds to the salad bowl. Drizzle with the dressing and toss well to combine. Sprinkle the remaining pomegranate seeds on top and serve.

Serves 4 to 6

FOR THE DRESSING:

2 tablespoons red wine vinegar

½ teaspoon kosher salt

½ teaspoon sugar

¼ cup (60 milliliters) extra-virgin olive oil

FOR THE SALAD:

2 bulbs fennel

1 cucumber

¼ cup (15 grams) roughly chopped fresh cilantro

¼ cup (15 grams) roughly chopped fresh parsley

2 tablespoons roughly chopped fresh mint

1 pomegranate

½ cup (60 grams) crumbled feta cheese

FRISÉE, BACON, DATE & QUAIL-EGG SALAD

Serves 4

FOR THE DRESSING:

4 ounces (115 grams) bacon, roughly chopped

1 shallot, halved and thinly sliced crosswise

3 dates, pitted and cut into rounds ¼ inch (6 millimeters) thick

2 tablespoons cider vinegar

1 large egg yolk

1 teaspoon Dijon mustard

¼ cup (60 milliliters) extra-virgin olive oil

FOR THE SALAD:

3 small heads frisée lettuce

8 quail eggs

3 dates, pitted and cut into rounds ¼ inch (6 millimeters) thick

Freshly ground black pepper

Crisp bacon bits and tiny quail eggs resting on a nest of frisée are an elegant, miniaturized version of a classic breakfast combo, making this salad perfect as a hearty brunch dish. The intense molasseslike sweetness of the dates and the rich bacon fat balance the bitter frisée.

1 *Make the dressing:* In a frying pan, cook the bacon over medium heat until completely crisp, about 10 minutes. Remove the bacon and drain on paper towels.

2 Add the shallot and dates to the pan and cook in the bacon fat until softened, about 1 minute. Remove from the heat and let cool slightly.

3 Combine the date-and-shallot mixture, vinegar, egg yolk, and mustard in a blender and blend until smooth. Add the oil and blend until just emulsified. Be careful not to blend too long, or the mixture will become very thick, like mayonnaise.

4 *Make the salad:* Cut off and discard the dark green parts of the frisée. Cut off the root and tear apart the pale green lettuce with your hands; you should have about 8 cups. Rinse with cold water and dry in a salad spinner. Place in a serving bowl.

5 Place the quail eggs in a small saucepan and cover with cold water. Bring to a boil, remove from the heat, and let sit for 3 minutes. Drain and rinse with cold water. Peel the eggs and halve them lengthwise; set aside.

6 Drizzle the salad with the dressing and toss very well to coat. Top with the reserved bacon, the dates, and the quail eggs. Season to taste with pepper and serve.

GREEK ISLAND SALAD

Served at every taverna in the Greek islands, this dish is nothing like the tepid Americanized version consisting of iceberg lettuce and anchovies. The Greek name, *horiatiki salata,* translates as "rustic salad," perfectly suiting this unfussy, tossed-together mixture of ripe summer vegetables and the trinity of salty Mediterranean ingredients—feta, olives, and capers. Serve with thick crusty bread to mop up the flavor-infused oil left in the bottom of the dish.

Serves 4 to 6

¼ red onion, thinly sliced

1 cucumber

4 ripe vine tomatoes

12 pitted kalamata olives

2 tablespoons drained capers

2 tablespoons red wine vinegar

¼ cup (60 milliliters) extra-virgin olive oil

4 ounces (115 grams) feta cheese, crumbled

1 teaspoon dried oregano

1   Place the onion in a bowl and cover with cold water. Let sit while you prepare the rest of the salad.

2   Partially peel the cucumber, leaving some strips of the dark green skin. Cut the cucumber in half lengthwise and cut into half rounds ½ inch (12 millimeters) thick.

3   Cut each tomato in half lengthwise and cut each half lengthwise into 4 wedges.

4   In a serving bowl, combine the cucumber, tomatoes, olives, and capers. Drain the onions, pat dry on paper towels, and add to the bowl.

5   In a separate small bowl, whisk together the vinegar and oil. Drizzle the dressing over the salad and toss to combine. Sprinkle with the cheese and oregano and serve.

LACINATO KALE SALAD

with Quick-Pickled Apple

Serves 4

FOR THE QUICK-PICKLED APPLE:

½ cup (120 milliliters) rice vinegar

3 tablespoons (35 grams) sugar

1 teaspoon kosher salt

1 tablespoon roughly chopped fresh dill

1 Macoun apple (or any medium-size crisp, semitart apple)

FOR THE DRESSING:

2 tablespoons freshly squeezed lemon juice (from 1 large lemon)

½ teaspoon honey

½ teaspoon kosher salt

¼ cup (60 milliliters) extra-virgin olive oil

FOR THE SALAD:

2 bunches lacinato kale, sometimes called cavolo nero or black kale (about 12 ounces / 340 grams)

Freshly ground black pepper

2 ounces (55 grams) aged pecorino Romano cheese

Lacinato kale is one of those foods that looks how it tastes; the deep velvety-green leaves knotted into complicated ridges echo the intensely vegetal, richly mineral taste. Served raw, the tough structure holds up to an acidic dressing without wilting. The quick-pickled apples lend a contrasting bite, both in crunch and flavor. Clean, simple, and satisfying.

1   *Make the quick-pickled apple:* In a medium-size bowl, combine the vinegar, sugar, salt, and dill and stir until the sugar and salt have dissolved. Halve the apple and scoop out the core (a standard metal measuring teaspoon works well for this). Cut crosswise into half rounds ⅛ inch (3 millimeters) thick. Add the apple rounds to the bowl with the vinegar mixture and toss. Let sit while you prepare the rest of the salad.

2   *Make the dressing:* In a small bowl or cup, combine the lemon juice, honey, and salt, and mix until the honey has dissolved. Add the oil and whisk with a fork until emulsified.

3   *Make the salad:* Trim and discard about 4 inches (10 centimeters) of the kale's thick stem ends. Slice the rest crosswise, as thinly as possible, so that you have long, thin ribbons. You should have about 8 cups (240 grams). Rinse well with cold water and dry in a salad spinner. Place in a large serving bowl.

4   Add a small splash of the pickling liquid to the bowl. Drain the apples and add them to the bowl. Add the dressing, season to taste with pepper, and toss to combine.

5   Using a mandoline, cheese shaver, or sharp paring knife, shave about half the cheese into the salad and toss to combine.

6   Let the salad marinate for a few minutes to soften the kale. Shave the rest of the cheese in a layer on top of the salad, top with more pepper, and serve.

MIXED-GREEN SALAD

with Plums

I love using fruit in savory dishes. Sometimes when preparing a meal I have to double-check that I've included at least one side that is fruit free. Plums pair beautifully with savory food and are a great match for wilder lettuces, their sweet flesh and naturally tart skins complementing the bitter undertones in the mixed greens while adding flashes of bright purple and gold to the salad. The raspberry balsamic dressing echoes the jammy, dark-fruit flavor of the plums.

1   *Make the dressing:* In a small bowl or cup, combine the vinegar, lemon juice, jam, and salt and mix well to dissolve. Add the oil and whisk with a fork until emulsified.

2   *Make the salad:* Remove any brown or damaged leaves from the romaine. Tear the rest into roughly 3-inch (7.5-centimeter) pieces and place in a large bowl.

3   Trim and discard the root end of the Bibb lettuce and gently break apart the leaves, discarding any brown bits. Tear the large leaves into roughly 3-inch (7.5-centimeter) pieces and combine with the romaine.

4   Trim and discard the root end of the radicchio and separate the leaves, discarding any old or brown pieces. Tear off and discard most of the dense white part of each leaf and add the purple bits to the rest of the lettuce.

5   Add the arugula to the bowl, cover with cold water, and toss to rinse. Drain and dry in a salad spinner. Transfer to a salad bowl or platter.

6   Cut the plums in half and remove the pits. Cut each half into 8 wedges. Add to the greens and toss to combine.

7   Just before serving, drizzle with the dressing and toss well to coat.

Serves 4 to 6

FOR THE DRESSING:

1 tablespoon plus 1 teaspoon balsamic vinegar

1 teaspoon freshly squeezed lemon juice (from ¼ small lemon)

2 teaspoons raspberry jam

½ teaspoon kosher salt

¼ cup (60 milliliters) extra-virgin olive oil

FOR THE SALAD:

1 head romaine lettuce

1 head Bibb lettuce

¼ small head red radicchio

1½ cups wild arugula (about 1 ounce / 30 grams)

2 red plums

RAW ROOT SALAD

Serves 4

FOR THE DRESSING:

2 tablespoons apple cider

1 tablespoon white wine vinegar

½ teaspoon kosher salt

3 tablespoons (45 milliliters)
extra-virgin olive oil

FOR THE SALAD:

2 medium parsnips (about 4 ounces /
115 grams), peeled

2 medium carrots (about 4 ounces /
115 grams), peeled

½ celery root, peeled

1 cup (30 grams) watercress

An elegant winter salad that combines the earthy sweetness of root vegetables with the peppery spice of watercress.

1 *Make the dressing:* In a small bowl or cup, combine the cider, vinegar, and salt and mix well to dissolve. Add the oil and whisk with a fork until emulsified.

2 *Make the salad:* Using a vegetable peeler, shave the parsnip into thin strips, discarding the center core. Repeat with the carrots and celery root. Place the shaved vegetables in a serving bowl.

3 Trim and discard the roots of the watercress, rinse, and dry in a salad spinner. Add the watercress to the shaved vegetables.

4 Drizzle with the dressing and toss well to combine.

ROMAINE HEARTS

with Buttermilk-Chive Dressing

This is my pared-down take on a Caesar salad. The creamy dressing is packed with fresh herbs for an intense springy flavor, but I also like the way the resulting vibrant green color looks against the pale greens and whites of the romaine hearts.

1   *Make the dressing:* In a blender, combine all the ingredients except the oil and blend on high speed until completely mixed. Add the oil and blend on high speed until completely combined. (The dressing can be stored, covered, in the refrigerator for several days. Stir before using.)

2   *Make the salad:* Remove any brown or wilted leaves from the romaine. Carefully trim the root ends of the hearts, leaving them attached so the leaves hold together. Quarter the hearts lengthwise (or halve the heads if using baby romaine) so that you have 8 wedges.

3   Arrange the wedges, cut side up, on a serving platter and drizzle with the dressing. Using a Microplane or the smallest holes on a box grater, grate the cheese over the salad and serve.

Serves 4

FOR THE DRESSING:

¼ cup (60 milliliters) buttermilk

2 tablespoons sour cream

2 tablespoons roughly chopped fresh parsley

1 heaping tablespoon chopped fresh chives

1 teaspoon freshly squeezed lime juice (from ½ small lime)

¼ teaspoon kosher salt

¼ teaspoon sugar

¼ cup (60 milliliters) grapeseed oil

FOR THE SALAD:

2 romaine lettuce hearts, or 4 heads baby romaine

2 ounces (55 grams) Parmesan cheese

GREEN SALAD

with Dill & Lemon Dressing

Serves 4 to 6

FOR THE DRESSING:

3 tablespoons (45 milliliters) lemon juice (from 1½ large lemons)

½ teaspoon kosher salt

¼ cup (60 milliliters) extra-virgin olive oil

FOR THE SALAD:

1 small head romaine lettuce

1 small head green-leaf lettuce

¼ cup (15 grams) roughly chopped fresh dill

2 tablespoons finely chopped fresh chives

This is my version of a classic Greek dish, *marouli salata,* which simply means lettuce salad. It's often served with sliced raw scallions but I substitute chives because they have a less overpowering bite. The freshness of the dill with the tangy lemon makes a great palate cleanser after a heavy or particularly rich meal.

1   *Make the dressing:* In a small bowl or cup, combine the lemon juice and salt and mix well to dissolve. Add the oil and whisk with a fork until emulsified.

2   *Make the salad:* Remove any brown or wilted outer leaves from both heads of lettuce. Cut the lettuce crosswise into ribbons about ½ inch (12 millimeters) thick. Rinse in cold water, drain, and dry in a salad spinner.

3   Place the lettuce in a large serving bowl. Add the dill and chives and toss to combine. Drizzle with the dressing, toss well, and serve.

SQUASH, BLOOD ORANGE & DANDELION GREENS

Raw dandelion greens are difficult to work with because they can be extremely bitter. Here, the honey-roasted sweetness from the squash and the rich, tongue-coating fats of the aged goat cheese balance out the bitterness for a complex, layered salad.

1   *Make the dressing:* In a small bowl or cup, combine the blood-orange juice, lemon juice, honey, and salt and mix well to combine. Add the oil and whisk with a fork until emulsified.

2   *Make the salad:* Preheat the oven to 400°F (205°C).

3   Halve the squash lengthwise; scoop out and discard the seeds. Cut into half rounds ½ inch (12 millimeters) thick, with the peel included.

4   In a bowl, toss the squash with the oil, honey, salt, cayenne, and black pepper to taste. Spread in a baking pan and roast until the squash is tender and slightly browned on the edges, about 30 minutes.

5   Trim and discard the thick stem ends of the greens, 3 to 4 inches (7.5 to 10 centimeters) off the bottom. Tear the remaining tender leaves into 2-inch (5-centimeter) pieces. Rinse well with cold water and dry.

6   Using a paring knife, cut off the ends of the blood oranges. Following the curve of the fruit with the knife, remove and discard the peel and white pith. Halve each orange and cut the halves into ½-inch (1.5-centimeter) thick rounds.

7   Arrange the greens on a platter. Top with the squash and sprinkle with the orange pieces. Drizzle with the dressing. Sprinkle with the pumpkin seeds and goat cheese and serve.

NOTE: To toast pumpkin seeds: Heat a small frying pan over high heat until very hot, about 1 minute. Add the pumpkin seeds and cook, stirring and tossing constantly, until they are lightly browned on both sides, 1 to 2 minutes. Remove from the heat, spread in a single layer, and let cool.

Serves 4

FOR THE DRESSING:

2 tablespoons freshly squeezed blood-orange juice (from 1 to 2 blood oranges)

1 teaspoon freshly squeezed lemon juice (from ¼ small lemon)

¼ teaspoon honey

¼ teaspoon kosher salt

3 tablespoons (45 milliliters) extra-virgin olive oil

FOR THE SALAD:

1 medium delicata squash (about 1 pound / 455 grams)

2 tablespoons extra-virgin olive oil

½ teaspoon honey

½ teaspoon kosher salt

Pinch of cayenne pepper

Freshly ground black pepper

¾ bunch dandelion greens (about 6 ounces / 170 grams)

2 blood oranges

3 tablespoons (20 grams) raw hulled pumpkins seeds (pepitas), toasted (see Note)

1 ounce (30 grams) garoxta or other firm aged Spanish goat cheese, very thinly shaved

TOMATO, NECTARINE & MOZZARELLA SALAD

The juicy, honey-sweet nectarine is just tart enough to play off the acidic, earthier tomato, while the mozzarella balances them both with fresh creaminess. Of course I can't help but love the visual impact of the overlapping bright reds, deep yellow, and milky white. A perfect salad for the height of August, when both fruits are at their peak, it should be served at room temperature to allow the flavors to mingle.

1   Cut the tomatoes crosswise into rounds ¼ inch (6 millimeters) thick.

2   Cut the nectarine in half vertically and remove the pit. Cut each half crosswise into half rounds ¼ inch (6 millimeters) thick.

3   Cut the cheese into half rounds ¼ inch (6 millimeters) thick.

4   Arrange the tomatoes, nectarine, and cheese on a platter, alternating and slightly overlapping each other.

5   Tear the basil leaves into ½-inch (12-millimeter) pieces and scatter over the salad.

6   Squeeze the juice from the lemon half and drizzle the oil over the salad.

7   Season with the salt and pepper to taste.

8   Let sit at room temperature for a few minutes before serving so that the juices combine.

Serves 4

3 ripe vine tomatoes (about 1 pound / 455 grams)

1 large ripe yellow nectarine

8 ounces (225 grams) fresh mozzarella cheese (half of a 1-pound ball)

6 fresh basil leaves

½ lemon

3 tablespoons (45 milliliters) extra-virgin olive oil

Heaping ¼ teaspoon kosher salt, or more to taste

Freshly ground black pepper

WATERMELON SALAD

Serves 4 to 6

FOR THE DRESSING:

2 tablespoons cider vinegar

½ teaspoon kosher salt

½ teaspoon sugar

¼ cup (60 milliliters) extra-virgin olive oil

FOR THE SALAD:

2 medium cucumbers (about 1 pound / 455 grams)

¼ small seedless watermelon (about 1½ pounds / 680 grams)

4 large stalks celery

5 red radishes

¼ cup (15 grams) roughly chopped fresh parsley

¼ teaspoon kosher salt, or more to taste

Freshly ground black pepper

In the tavernas on Hydra, at the end of a big meal the kitchen will often send out a complimentary plate of *karpouzi*, the Greek word for "watermelon," sliced off the rind into large chunks and simply stuck with as many forks as there are people at your table. As a result, I've developed a Pavlovian craving for that refreshing sweet crunch whenever meals draw to an end. While unadorned juicy watermelon is as pure a treat as you're going to get, it can also be a delicious addition to salads, contributing a dimension of sweetness without being cloying. I'm afraid that watermelon salad has been veering into cliché territory in restaurants, as one of those ingredients that gets tossed in with something incongruous just because it sounds nice on a menu. Here, I think the mild flavors and varied crunchiness of the celery, cucumber, radish, and watermelon blend together seamlessly, just as their colors create a beautiful mix of pinks and pale greens.

1   *Make the dressing:* In a small bowl or cup, combine the vinegar, salt, and sugar and mix well to dissolve. Add the oil and whisk with a fork until emulsified.

2   *Make the salad:* Peel the cucumbers and cut them in half lengthwise. Using a spoon, scoop out and discard the seeds. Cut into crescents ¼ inch (6 millimeters) thick.

3   Cut off and discard the watermelon rind. Cut the watermelon into roughly 1-inch (2.5-centimeter) cubes; you should have about 3 cups (450 grams).

4   Peel the outside of the celery. Trim off and discard about 1 inch from the bottom of each stalk, then cut the rest into slices ¼ inch (6 millimeters) thick. Reserve ½ cup (20 grams) of the pale tender celery leaves.

5   Trim off and discard the ends of the radishes and cut them into very thin rounds.

6   In a large bowl, combine the cucumbers, watermelon, celery, and radishes and add the parsley and the celery leaves. Drizzle with the dressing and toss well to combine. Season with the salt and pepper to taste. Toss again and serve.

SCLAFANI
All Natural
Made From
Fresh Ripe
Tomatoes
NET WT. 28 OZ. (1 LB. 12 OZ.)
CRUSHED TOMATOES
ICES

Every day at The Smile we put together two different soup specials, one for the lunch crowd and one for dinner. "Soup of the Day" is an age-old restaurant trick that everyone uses to get rid of produce that's on its way out, or to give a second life to leftover ingredients. Despite those humble origins, our soups have often been among my favorite dishes on the menu. There's something to be said for a total lack of premeditation and a casual throw-it-in-the-pot attitude.

4
SOUPS

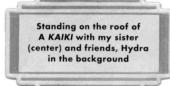

**Standing on the roof of
A KAIKI with my sister
(center) and friends, Hydra
in the background**

I find that great recipes can be born out of intuitively combining ingredients that you happen to have on hand—wouldn't a roasted pear go nicely in this butternut squash soup? Why don't we sauté some fennel in there and see how it tastes? When it comes to soup, I like a bold, uncomplicated flavor that will be instantly satisfying from the first spoonful. As often as possible, I try to make the soup of the day vegetarian-friendly (or even vegan-friendly, since we're already halfway there). Yes, there are many great soups that cannot do without the rich, meaty flavor of homemade beef broth or chicken stock, but in this chapter I've focused on vegetarian soups with pure, straightforward ingredients. I start with the extremely simple formula of melted onions, a vegetable, water, and salt. From there I tweak by adding complementary flavors—an aromatic bay leaf to give subtlety to a combination of potato and leeks, a squeeze of lime to cut the sweetness of the butternut, a few carrots to bulk up the tomatoes.

At home, I like to make a batch of soup, keep it in the fridge, and heat it up over the course of a week. For a quick lunch by myself, I'll have a cup of soup and a simple salad. For dinner I'll bring a bubbling saucepan to the table with a few garnishes—a bunch of cilantro sprigs or a small pitcher of chili oil. We'll ladle the soup into bowls at the table and enjoy it with the rest of the meal. Soup is by its nature casual and rustic, food in its most immediate and comforting form. It can be soothing and warm in the winter and, as in the case of gazpacho, refreshing and cool in the summer.

ROASTED-TOMATO SOUP

Tomato soup is the essential taste of childhood for so many who were raised on Campbell's classic version. Since I didn't grow up with it I never craved it, but then one of my cooks, Sammy, developed a version of this recipe to go with our grilled cheese sandwich special. It was an instant hit with customers (and with me). The roasting intensifies the tomato flavor, while the fennel adds a barely detectable note of anise.

1 Preheat the oven to 400°F (205°C).

2 In a large roasting pan, combine the tomatoes with ½ teaspoon of the salt, pepper to taste, and 2 tablespoons (30 milliliters) of the oil. Toss well to coat. Roast until the tomatoes are completely soft and some are slightly browned at the edges, about 30 minutes.

3 Meanwhile, remove the darkest green top of the leek and trim the root end. Cut in half lengthwise and rinse well under cold running water, peeling back the layers to remove any dirt. Thinly slice crosswise.

4 Trim the top and root end of the fennel, cut the bulb in half, and remove the tough outer layer and dense white core. Slice very thinly crosswise.

5 In a deep saucepan, heat the remaining 2 tablespoons (30 milliliters) oil over medium-high heat for 30 seconds. Add the leek, fennel, onion, and carrots. Cook, stirring occasionally, until the vegetables are soft and slightly caramelized, about 10 minutes.

6 Add the tomatoes and any juices from the roasting pan to the pot and mix well. Add 3 cups (720 milliliters) water and stir. Bring to a simmer and cook for at least 10 minutes for the flavors to combine. Remove from the heat and let cool slightly.

7 Transfer the soup to a blender or food processor, in batches as necessary, and blend on high speed until completely smooth. Return the soup to the pot and taste for seasoning; add the remaining ½ teaspoon salt or more, if desired. Season with pepper to taste. Cook over medium heat until bubbling hot.

8 Ladle into bowls and serve.

Makes about 6 cups (1.4 liters); serves 4

5 ripe vine tomatoes (about 2 pounds / 910 grams), roughly chopped into 1-inch (2.5-centimeter) pieces

1 teaspoon kosher salt, divided, or more to taste

Freshly ground black pepper

4 tablespoons (60 milliliters) extra-virgin olive oil, divided

1 large leek

1 fennel bulb

1 yellow onion, cut into ½-inch (12-millimeter) pieces

2 carrots, peeled and diced

GAZPACHO

Makes about 6 cups (1.4 liters); serves 4

10 ripe vine tomatoes (3 to 4 pounds / 1.4 to 1.8 kilograms)

2 cucumbers (about 1½ pounds / 680 grams), peeled, seeded, and roughly chopped

1½ red bell peppers, seeded and roughly chopped

½ yellow onion, roughly chopped (about 1 cup)

¾ cup (180 milliliters) extra-virgin olive oil

3 cloves garlic, pressed or finely minced

2 tablespoons red wine vinegar

2 teaspoons kosher salt, or more to taste

After I graduated from college, I celebrated by taking a trip to Spain—but without doing enough research. I foolishly went to Seville in the dead of summer, when every local with any sense had left town to avoid the paralyzing heat. I kept my body temperature down by seeking out a bowl of delicious chilled gazpacho every few hours. Looking back, I realize the gazpacho trail was one of my favorite experiences, and I've mentally blocked out the molasses-thick summer air in favor of a succession of cooling, tangy, tomato-red purees. Every restaurant has its own take on gazpacho. Personally I like it smooth rather than diced (which is too much like salsa for my taste). I can't imagine a list of ingredients combining more perfectly than those in a classic gazpacho, with its seamless blending of flavors.

1   Cut the tomatoes in half crosswise. Remove and discard stem ends. Scoop out and discard the seeds and roughly chop the rest.

2   In a large bowl, combine the tomatoes, cucumbers, peppers, onion, oil, garlic, vinegar, and salt and toss to combine. Let sit for at least 5 minutes for the salt to draw out the juices and to allow the flavors to combine.

3   Working in batches, transfer the mixture to a blender or food processor and blend on high speed until completely smooth. Return to the bowl, taste for seasoning, and add more salt, if desired.

4   Chill for at least 30 minutes before serving.

POTATO-LEEK SOUP

There's something about this classic French soup that feels at once austere and elegant. I can imagine a family of Provençal farmers sitting around a worn wooden table eating this melted mixture of pale green leeks and hearty potatoes out of impossibly beautiful white bowls. That little fantasy sums up what I think of this dish—filling, wholesome, yet lovely in its simplicity.

Makes about 7 cups; serves 4

2 medium russet potatoes (about 1½ pounds / 680 grams)

2 large leeks (about 1 pound / 455 grams)

1 fennel bulb

2 tablespoons extra-virgin olive oil

2 tablespoons unsalted butter

2 cloves garlic, pressed or finely minced

3 stalks celery, thinly sliced

1 bay leaf

1 teaspoon kosher salt, or more to taste

⅛ teaspoon ground white pepper, or more to taste

Reduced cream (optional; see Note)

Freshly ground black pepper

1   Add cold water to a large bowl. Peel the potatoes and cut them into ½-inch (12-millimeter) chunks, covering them in the water while you prepare the rest of the ingredients.

2   Remove the darkest green tops of the leeks and trim the root ends. Cut in half lengthwise and rinse well under cold running water, peeling back the layers to remove any dirt. Thinly slice crosswise.

3   Trim the top and root end of the fennel, cut in half, and remove the tough outer layer and dense white core. Slice very thinly crosswise.

4   In a deep pot, heat the oil and butter over medium-high heat. Add the garlic and cook for 30 seconds. Add the leeks, fennel, and celery and cook, stirring often, until the vegetables are completely soft but not browned at all, 5 to 7 minutes.

5   Drain the potatoes and add them to the pot. Stir to coat with the leek mixture. Add 4 cups (480 milliliters) water, the bay leaf, 1 teaspoon salt, and ⅛ teaspoon white pepper. Cover, reduce the heat to medium, and cook until the potatoes are completely soft and falling apart, about 30 minutes.

6   Taste for seasoning and add more salt and white pepper, if desired. Remove and discard the bay leaf. I like to serve the soup rustic style—with a thick, chunky texture—but you can also puree it at this point if you prefer. Drizzle each serving with about 1 tablespoon reduced cream, if desired, sprinkle with black pepper, then serve.

NOTE: To make reduced cream: In a small saucepan, heat ½ cup (120 milliliters) heavy cream over medium-low heat. Bring to a simmer and cook until reduced by half, about 3 minutes. Keep watching carefully, because cream can boil over very fast—usually the minute you turn your back.

MOROCCAN TOMATO-VEGETABLE SOUP

Makes about 7 cups (1.7 liters); serves 4

½ large butternut squash (about 1½ pounds / 680 grams)

2 tablespoons extra-virgin olive oil

1 yellow onion, cut into ½-inch (12-millimeter) pieces

2 stalks celery, thinly sliced

1 yellow potato, cut into ½-inch (12-millimeter) pieces

1 carrot, peeled and cut into ¼-inch (6-millimeter) thick rounds

1 teaspoon kosher salt, or more to taste

Freshly ground black pepper

5 ripe vine tomatoes (about 2 pounds / 910 grams), roughly chopped

½ cup (30 grams) roughly chopped fresh cilantro, plus more for garnish

1 teaspoon sugar

2 teaspoons *ras el hanout* (see Note)

¼ teaspoon turmeric

¼ teaspoon ground coriander

About ¼ cup (65 grams) plain Greek yogurt

This is my favorite mixed-vegetable soup for a cold day, chunky and satisfying, subtly warmed by the Moroccan spice blend *ras el hanout*. The dollop of tangy yogurt on top is a must; it brings the hearty vegetables together with a nice contrasting sharpness and hint of cream.

1   Peel the squash, and remove and discard the seeds. Chop into ½-inch (12-millimeter) cubes; you should have about 4 cups (568 grams).

2   In a deep pot, heat the oil over medium-high heat for 30 seconds.

3   Add the onion and celery. Cook, stirring, until softened but not browned, about 5 minutes.

4   Add the squash, potato, and carrot. Season with the salt and pepper to taste. Cook, stirring occasionally, until softened, about 8 minutes.

5   Add the tomatoes and cook, stirring occasionally, until they have broken down and released their juices, about 10 minutes.

6   Add 2 cups (480 milliliters) water, the cilantro, sugar, *ras el hanout*, turmeric, and coriander. Bring to a simmer and cook, stirring occasionally, until all the vegetables are completely tender, about 15 minutes. Season to taste with more salt and pepper, if desired.

7   Ladle into bowls, top each with a spoonful of yogurt, sprinkle with more cilantro, and serve.

NOTE: *Ras el hanout* is a Moroccan spice mixture that can be found in better supermarkets and specialty stores, as well as online. Each blend is different, but it will usually include coriander, cumin, cinnamon, cloves, and cardamom.

ROASTED-BUTTERNUT SQUASH SOUP

Makes about 6 cups (1.4 liters); serves 4

1 medium butternut squash (about 3 pounds / 1.4 kilograms)

1 green pear, such as Anjou or Bartlett

6 tablespoons (90 milliliters) extra-virgin olive oil, divided

1 teaspoon kosher salt

Freshly ground black pepper

1 yellow onion, cut into ½-inch (12-millimeter) pieces

½ teaspoon ground coriander

Pinch of cayenne pepper

1 tablespoon freshly squeezed lime juice (from 1 lime)

Heavy cream (optional)

As the last heat of summer has faded and the leaves start changing, I know it's really fall when I start craving a comforting bowl of bright-orange butternut squash soup. The danger with naturally creamy butternut is that it can be cloyingly sweet and too uniform after a few spoonfuls. To cut that sweetness, I add a pinch of cayenne and splash of lime juice. I also like to add a pear during the roasting stage to give a little texture and a slight floral aroma.

1   Preheat the oven to 400°F (205°C). Line a baking sheet with aluminum foil.

2   Peel the squash, cut it in half lengthwise, and scoop out and discard the seeds. Cut into roughly 1-inch (2.5-centimeter) pieces.

3   Halve the pear lengthwise and remove the core and the stem end. Cut into roughly 1-inch (2.5-centimeter) pieces.

4   Combine the squash and pear on the prepared baking sheet. Drizzle with ¼ cup (60 milliliters) of the oil and season with the salt and pepper to taste. Toss well to coat and spread in a single layer. Roast until the squash is completely tender and has browned slightly on the edges, about 1 hour.

5   In a deep saucepan, heat the remaining 2 tablespoons (30 milliliters) oil over medium-high heat for 30 seconds. Add the onion, coriander, and cayenne. Cook, stirring occasionally, until the onion is soft and translucent but not browned, about 5 minutes.

The difference between just eating food and enjoying a meal is often in the details. My advice is to dine by candlelight whenever you can. It sounds silly, but as every restaurant owner and successful party host knows, lighting accounts for 90 percent of setting the right atmosphere. Everything and everyone looks a little better in the warm glow of candlelight, and it shouldn't be relegated to the clichéd "romantic" dinner. Even if I'm just eating a quick thrown-together meal alone with my husband, we always set the table, dim the lamps, and light a few candles. I have a range of different-size vintage candlesticks permanently set on the table and I keep a variety of unscented colored tapers on hand. If you don't have candlesticks, you can improvise—set the mood for a tagine feast using jewel-toned Moroccan tea glasses as votives. For a pared-down DIY look, take a few old glass jars, drip a bit of wax from a candle into the bottom of each jar, and stick a long taper onto the hot wax so that it stays upright.

6   Add the squash and pear and any oil from the roasting pan. Cook, stirring, until well combined, 1 to 2 minutes. Add 4 cups (960 milliliters) water and bring to a simmer. Cook, uncovered, for 10 minutes.

7   Remove from the heat and let cool slightly. Transfer the soup to a blender or food processor, in batches as necessary, and blend on high speed until completely smooth.

8   Return the soup to the saucepan and stir in the lime juice. Taste for seasoning. Add more salt and pepper if desired. Cook over medium heat until bubbling hot. Stir in a splash of cream here if you prefer a richer soup.

9   Ladle into bowls and serve.

It's not an accident that there are more recipes in this chapter than in any other in the book: Vegetables are my favorite food to cook. They offer such a boundless variety of taste, color, and texture that I'm still discovering new vegetables and learning to appreciate the ones I wrote off when I was younger. There are countless ways to prepare even one vegetable, let alone the whole cornucopia; I could fill a book with string-bean recipes if I wanted to. I love the immediacy and constant interaction of sautéing or simmering vegetables on the stovetop; you get a feel for the way the flavor is developing by watching the changing appearance and smelling the aroma wafting from your pan, seasoning and adjusting as you go.

5
VEGETABLES & STARCHES

This chapter is full of the easy and flavorful recipes that I end up returning to again and again—simple sautéed greens finished with a splash of cider vinegar, rosemary-infused honey-glazed carrots, golden mashed potatoes with capers and fresh dill. The ingredients seem to melt into each other, creating something utterly different from those same foods in their raw state. A trip to a greenmarket or a well-stocked grocery store is always inspiring to me—towers of shapes and shades, bountiful greens, bright oranges, and the deep red of freshly pulled beets. When I'm making dinner at home I don't usually plan ahead; I just go to the market and see what jumps out at me—a particularly appetizing batch of plump green string beans, perhaps, or the first shipment of slender spring asparagus. Here, I've tried to provide a full range of recipes, with something for every season—squash, iron-rich leafy dark greens, and sweet, earthy roots during the cold months; young, fresh, ripe-tasting vegetables like zucchini and lusciously sweet corn during the warmer months.

When I'm cooking at home I don't often stick to the model of a meat dish, a vegetable, and a starch. More often than not, I'll cook a meat or a fish and two or three different vegetables, including a darker green and something else with a nicely contrasting but complementary flavor. It's not that I don't love rice, potatoes, couscous, and pasta; I just don't buy into the vaguely 1950s American concept of a balanced menu that includes starch by default. Starches work beautifully when they are essential to the rest of the meal—fragrant, fluffy couscous absorbing the rich broth of a stew, or crisp potatoes mirroring the darkened skin of a roasted chicken. To me the ideal dinner emulates a luxurious Mediterranean spread, where you can sample a variety of tastes and textures. I think of my family ordering in a Greek taverna, shouting over each other to secure our favorite choices from the kitchen. The result is a banquet of flavors: roasted eggplant, stuffed tomatoes, and the distinctive bitter green *horta*. Everything is meant to be enjoyed family style over a long, relaxed meal.

That said, I can't help but have an enormous soft spot for potatoes. Despite the fact that they're actually quite nutritious, they've gotten a bad reputation in recent years from carbphobic dieters. I believe the real reason potatoes can put such a dent in your diet is that they're so often drowned in cheese, cream, and butter. It's almost impossible to discern their natural earthy sweetness when they are overwhelmed with intensely fatty flavors. I've included a few recipes that highlight the actual flavor of the potato rather than the taste of a stick of butter. But it's their transformative texture that is the real revelation—uniquely fluffy and naturally creamy when mashed, crisp on the outside and deliciously dense on the inside when roasted.

BOILED DANDELION GREENS

Horta is a wild dark bitter green that grows well in Greece's sun-drenched, rocky terrain. Simply boiled and dressed with olive oil and lemon, it has a rich, mineral-like flavor and is a staple in almost every Greek restaurant. Dandelion greens are the closest equivalent widely available in the United States; they are a clean-tasting accompaniment to roasted meats and grilled fish.

1   Rinse the greens very well and trim off the root ends. Pick out and discard any brown or wilted leaves.

2   Add the 2 teaspoons salt and the vinegar to a large pot of water and bring it to a boil. Add the greens and cook until they are very tender but still green and not completely wilted, about 8 minutes.

3   Drain the greens and let them cool enough to handle (you can rinse with lukewarm water to stop the greens from cooking). Roughly chop into 1-inch (2.5-centimeter) pieces, transfer to a serving platter, and drizzle with the oil and lemon juice. Season to taste with salt and pepper.

Serves 4

3 bunches dandelion greens (1¼ to 1½ pounds / 570 to 680 grams)

2 teaspoons kosher salt, or more to taste

1 teaspoon distilled white vinegar

¼ cup (60 milliliters) extra-virgin olive oil

2 tablespoons freshly squeezed lemon juice (from 1 large lemon)

Freshly ground black pepper

BRUSSELS SPROUTS

with Bacon & Pomegranate Seeds

Serves 4

1 pomegranate

1 pound (455 grams) Brussels sprouts

Kosher salt

4 ounces (115 grams) bacon (about 4 strips), cut into pieces ½ inch (12 millimeters) wide

2 shallots, finely minced

1 tablespoon fresh thyme leaves

Kosher salt

Freshly ground black pepper

Brussels sprouts have become an American staple, earning a place in the pantheon of Thanksgiving side dishes that get reimagined in food magazines and on blogs every year as November rolls around. The densely packed bundles of leaves absorb bold flavors, especially when roasting or pan-searing mellows their cabbagelike aroma into a rich sweetness. In my version, the dark, fruity flavor and acidity of the pomegranate seeds cut through the rich fattiness of the bacon.

1   Cut the pomegranate in half and reserve one half for another use. Hold the fruit over a bowl and hit it with the back of a wooden spoon to knock the seeds out. Pick out any bits of white membrane that stick to the seeds. You should have about ½ cup (60 grams) seeds.

2   Trim the root ends off the Brussels sprouts and cut them in half lengthwise. Remove any brown outer leaves.

3   Bring a pot of salted water to a boil. Add the Brussels sprouts and cook until just tender, about 5 minutes. Drain and rinse with cold water to stop them from cooking and set aside.

4   In a heavy-bottomed sauté pan, cook the bacon over medium heat until it is brown and crisp and most of the fat has been rendered out into the pan, about 10 minutes. Remove from the heat.

5   Remove the bacon from the pan and set aside; drain off and discard about 1 tablespoon of the fat and leave the rest in the pan.

6   Return the pan to medium-high heat. Add the shallots and thyme and cook, scraping up the browned bits from the bottom of the pan, until the shallots are just turning golden.

7   Add the Brussels sprouts, ¼ teaspoon salt, and pepper to taste. Cook, stirring often, until the sprouts are warmed through and slightly browned. Add the bacon and stir well to combine.

8   Transfer to a serving bowl, sprinkle with the pomegranate seeds, and serve.

EGGPLANT CAPONATA

I have a bit of a sweet tooth when it comes to savory food. The alchemy of caramelized onions is one of my favorite elements of cooking—all that assertively pungent crispness melting into rich, buttery sweetness. That sweetness is the backbone of this dish, a complement to the smoky flesh and tannic dark skin of the eggplant. It's very important that you roast the eggplant mixture long enough for the onions and tomatoes to really get that good dark golden flavor (my advice is to err on the side of burning rather than undercooking). This recipe can be served warm as a vegetable side dish, blending with other flavors and textures on your plate, but it also tastes delicious served cold the next day on a sandwich or as a spread.

1   Preheat the oven to 400°F (205°C).

2   Cut off and discard the stem ends of the eggplants. Cut the eggplants into ½-inch (12-millimeter) cubes.

3   Cut the grape tomatoes in half lengthwise.

4   Dice the onion into ½-inch (12-millimeter) pieces.

5   In a large roasting pan, combine the eggplant, tomatoes, onion, and garlic. The pan should be large enough to spread the mixture in one even layer; if the eggplant cubes are overlapping too much, they will steam in the oven instead of roasting and won't be as flavorful.

6   Drizzle with the honey, season with the salt and pepper to taste, and pour the oil over all. Toss well to combine.

7   Roast until the edges of the eggplant and tomatoes are browned and the onions are slightly caramelized, at least 1 hour.

8   Add the parsley. Mix well with a spoon, mashing the eggplant and tomato together as you stir. Transfer to a bowl and serve.

Serves 4

2 eggplants (about 2 pounds / 910 grams)

1 pint (300 grams) grape tomatoes

1 medium red onion

3 cloves garlic, pressed or finely minced

2 teaspoons honey

1 teaspoon kosher salt

Freshly ground black pepper

½ cup plus 2 tablespoons (150 milliliters) extra-virgin olive oil

¼ cup (15 grams) roughly chopped fresh parsley

SPICY CAULIFLOWER

with Saffron, Honey & Capers

Serves 4

⅛ teaspoon crumbled saffron

1 head cauliflower (about 2 pounds / 910 grams)

2 shallots

3 tablespoons (45 milliliters) extra-virgin olive oil

1 cheek of a habanero pepper (or any spicy red chili), thinly sliced

¼ cup (30 grams) capers

1 teaspoon honey

¾ teaspoon kosher salt

Freshly ground black pepper

¼ cup (15 grams) roughly chopped fresh parsley

Cauliflower, with its pale color and lightly musky taste, is built to take on bolder flavors. Here, the creamy florets create a backdrop for the brash regal saffron, intense briny capers, and habanero kick.

1   In a small bowl, combine the saffron with ¾ cup (180 milliliters) warm water and let sit while you prepare the rest of the ingredients.

2   Trim the tough outer leaves from the cauliflower. Cut in half, cut off and discard the dense white interior stem, and break the cauliflower into 1-inch (2.5-centimeter) florets.

3   Cut the shallots in half lengthwise and cut the halves lengthwise into wedges ¼ inch (6 millimeters) thick.

4   In a wide sauté pan, heat the oil over medium-high heat for 30 seconds. Add the shallots and cook until softened and just turning golden around the edges, 1 to 2 minutes. Add the habanero, capers, and honey and cook until the shallots are browned, about 2 more minutes.

5   Add the cauliflower, salt, and black pepper to taste. Cook, stirring, until the cauliflower is well coated with the shallot mixture.

6   Add the saffron water and stir to coat. Cover, reduce the heat to medium, and cook until all the water has been absorbed and the cauliflower is tender, about 12 minutes.

7   Uncover, sprinkle with the parsley, and serve.

GRILLED ASPARAGUS

with Preserved Lemon

Serves 4

1½ bunches asparagus (about 1½ pounds / 680 grams), rinsed

2 tablespoons plus 2 teaspoons (40 milliliters) extra-virgin olive oil, divided

½ teaspoon kosher salt

Freshly ground black pepper

1 half preserved lemon (see page 36)

Here's a quick vegetable dish to whip together when you've got the grill going. The preserved lemon is an earthier alternative to brightly acidic lemon zest.

1   Snap the woody ends off the asparagus where they break naturally. Trim the ends so that they're even (or don't, if you're not feeling fussy).

2   In a large bowl, toss the asparagus with 2 tablespoons (30 milliliters) of the oil, the salt, and pepper to taste.

3   Scoop out and discard the flesh of the lemon half. Dice the skin very finely and place in a serving dish that will accommodate the asparagus. Drizzle with the remaining 2 teaspoons (10 milliliters) oil.

4   Preheat a charcoal or gas grill to medium-high. Place the asparagus on the grill over indirect heat (around the edges, away from the flame). Cook until tender and slightly charred, turning to cook both sides, about 6 minutes per side.

5   Remove to the prepared serving dish. Toss to coat with the preserved lemon and serve.

GRILLED CORN

with Lime Butter

Summer corn grilled in its husk is so succulent it's hard to improve on. Having said that, here the zestiness of the lime and the creaminess of the butter add extra dimensions of flavor to the corn's natural sweetness.

1   In a small bowl, mix the butter, zest, and juice until well combined. Press the mixture into another small bowl and smooth the top with a knife. Wipe off the sides of the bowl with a paper towel. Refrigerate until hard, at least 20 minutes.

2   Preheat a charcoal or gas grill to medium-high. Place the corn directly on the grill and cook until the husk is blackened, about 15 minutes. Turn and cook until the rest of the husk is blackened as well, 10 to 15 more minutes.

3   Serve with the lime butter. Let your guests peel back the husks and add butter to taste.

Serves 4

½ cup (1 stick / 115 grams) salted butter, softened

Finely grated zest of 1 lime

1 teaspoon freshly squeezed lime juice (from ½ small lime)

4 ears corn, in their husks

ROASTED BEETS

As an adult I love beets for the same reason I hated them as a child: they taste like dirt. Now I see that as a positive; their full earthiness reminds me of the smell of rainwater on a forest floor, sweet and mossy as well as dark and minerally. The great thing about roasted beets, simply flavored with a few thyme leaves, is that they're almost impossible to overcook. Their flavor just intensifies the longer you leave them in the oven.

1   Place the beets in a large pot, cover with cold water, and add the ½ teaspoon salt. Bring to a boil and cook until the beets are tender, about 30 minutes. Drain.

2   As soon as the beets are cool enough to handle, rub off their skins using a paper towel or a dishcloth; don't let them cool completely or they will be harder to peel.

3   Cut each beet lengthwise into wedges 1 inch (2.5 centimeters) wide.

4   Preheat the oven to 400°F (205°C). Line a baking sheet with aluminum foil.

5   Place the beets on the baking sheet, drizzle with the oil, add the thyme, season with additional salt and pepper to taste, and toss to coat. Roast until some of the edges are slightly browned, at least 30 minutes. Serve.

Serves 4

3 to 4 red beets (about 1 pound / 455 grams), with tops and greens removed

3 to 4 gold beets (about 1 pound / 455 grams), with tops and greens removed

½ teaspoon kosher salt, plus more to taste

2 tablespoons extra-virgin olive oil

1 tablespoon fresh thyme leaves

Freshly ground black pepper

ROASTED FAIRYTALE EGGPLANTS

with Spicy Lime Yogurt Sauce

Serves 4

2 pounds (910 grams) fairytale eggplants, halved lengthwise (see Note)

6 tablespoons (90 milliliters) extra-virgin olive oil

1 teaspoon kosher salt

Freshly ground black pepper

Spicy Lime Yogurt Sauce (page 117)

Chopped fresh mint (optional)

I first experimented with this dish when I was working in a restaurant on the Caribbean island of St. Barts. Because the island is a French municipality, the supermarkets are amazing, filled with classic French delicacies, incredible cheeses, cured ham, and champagne, as well as small but well-curated selections of produce. After work I would wander through my local supermarket and put together the elements of a simple dinner to cook in the limited kitchen at my rented beach cottage. That's where I first picked up these pale purple beauties—slender, miniature eggplants laced with a delicate white brushstroke pattern on their skins. Their dense flesh is creamier than that of their larger cousins. Because they're small, they have a higher skin-to-flesh ratio, which helps them hold their shape when roasted or grilled. Now I often see them cropping up in supermarkets or farm stands in the United States.

1   Preheat the oven to 425°F (220°C). Line a baking sheet with aluminum foil.

2   Trim the stem ends off the eggplants and cut in half lengthwise. Place on the baking sheet. Toss with the oil, salt, and pepper to taste until well coated.

3   Spread the eggplants in an even layer, cut side down, and roast until browned and crisp, 20 to 30 minutes.

4   Serve with a bowl of the yogurt sauce (page 117). You can also spoon the sauce on top of the eggplants and sprinkle with the chopped mint, if desired.

NOTE: If you can't find fairytale eggplants, use the smallest eggplants you can find and cut them into wedges 1 inch (2.5 centimeters) thick and 2 inches (5 centimeters) long.

SPICY LIME YOGURT SAUCE

1   In a small bowl, combine the lime juice and chili and let sit for at least 10 minutes. Strain the juice into another bowl and discard the chili.

2   Add the yogurt, oil, ¼ cup (25 grams) mint, garlic, and salt and mix well.

3   To serve, sprinkle with the remaining 1 tablespoon mint.

Makes about 1 cup (240 milliliters)

2 tablespoons freshly squeezed lime juice (from 2 limes)

1 Thai red chili, cut in half lengthwise

1 cup (250 grams) plain Greek yogurt

2 tablespoons extra-virgin olive oil

¼ cup (25 grams) plus 1 tablespoon finely chopped fresh mint, divided

1 clove garlic, pressed or finely minced

½ teaspoon kosher salt

ROSEMARY-&-HONEY-GLAZED CARROTS

Serves 4

12 carrots (about 1½ pounds / 680 grams), tops removed, peeled

4 sprigs fresh rosemary

1 teaspoon kosher salt, or more to taste

1 tablespoon unsalted butter

2 teaspoons honey

Freshly ground black pepper

This was my mom's go-to vegetable dish when I was growing up—an uncomplicated preparation that's easy to like. The carrots are infused with the rosemary flavor and then lightly glazed with butter and honey.

1   Place the carrots and rosemary in a wide sauté pan, cover with about ½ inch (12 millimeters) cold water, and add the salt.

2   Bring to a boil over high heat and cook until the carrots are just tender, about 8 minutes, depending on the size of your carrots.

3   Remove from the heat. Drain off the water, leaving the carrots in the pan, and discard the rosemary. (You can prepare everything up to this point in advance and finish the rest just before you serve.)

4   Add the butter and honey and return the pan to high heat. Cook until the carrots are well coated with melted butter and warmed through. Season with pepper and more salt to taste, if desired, and serve.

SWEET & SPICY SAUTÉED LACINATO KALE

Serves 4

3 bunches lacinato kale (about 1½ pounds / 680 grams)

1 large Vidalia onion (about 1 pound / 455 grams)

2 red Fresno chilies, or any medium-spicy red chili about the size of a jalapeño

3 tablespoons (45 milliliters) extra-virgin olive oil

½ teaspoon kosher salt, or more to taste

½ teaspoon honey

Freshly ground black pepper

1 tablespoon cider vinegar

The dark green mineral taste of the kale is nicely balanced by the sweetness of the caramelized onions and mellow spice of the chilies. The tough ridged leaves hold their structure instead of completely wilting when cooked like spinach or chard, giving the dish a nice fullness.

1   Trim off and discard about 4 inches (10 centimeters) of the kale's thick stem ends. Cut the rest crosswise into ribbons ½ inch (12 millimeters) thick. It will seem like a lot, but it cooks down very quickly in the pan. Wash with cold water, drain, and set aside.

2   Cut the onion in half lengthwise, then thinly slice crosswise.

3   Cut the chilies in half lengthwise and remove the seeds and white core. Thinly slice crosswise and combine with the onion.

4   In a wide heavy-bottomed sauté pan, heat the oil over medium-high heat for 30 seconds. Add the onion and chilies and cook, stirring often, until the onion is golden and caramelized, 8 to 10 minutes.

5   Add the kale in batches; allow each batch to cook down a bit and make room in the pan for more. Add the salt, drizzle with honey, and season to taste with pepper. Cook, stirring to incorporate the onions, until the kale is wilted and soft but still bright green, 2 to 3 minutes.

6   Add the vinegar, cook for 30 seconds, remove from the heat, taste for seasoning, and serve.

SAUTÉED SUMMER SQUASH

When I'm not sure what to cook, I always return to the reliable combination of crushed chilies, garlic, and squash. When they're in season, summer squash are a bright golden yellow, dense and meaty, with a slight sweetness. Quickly sautéed and sprinkled with refreshing mint, this makes for a simple summer dish with big flavor.

1   In a wide heavy-bottomed sauté pan, heat the oil over medium heat for 30 seconds. Add the garlic and cook, stirring constantly, until it just turns golden around the edges, 1 to 2 minutes.

2   Add the squash, salt, and chili flakes. Season with the pepper to taste and cook, stirring, until just tender, about 4 minutes.

3   Remove from the heat, let cool slightly, and stir in the mint before serving.

Serves 4

3 tablespoons (45 milliliters) extra-virgin olive oil

2 cloves garlic, very thinly sliced

4 small to medium summer squash (about 1¼ pounds / 570 grams), cut into ⅛-inch (3-millimeter) thick rounds

½ teaspoon kosher salt

¼ teaspoon red chili flakes

Freshly ground black pepper

2 tablespoons finely chopped fresh mint

SEARED FENNEL WEDGES

with Orange Dressing

I like to serve this dish at room temperature, like a traditional Italian antipasto. The fennel also tastes delicious grilled, but I prefer the more intensely caramelized edges you get from pan searing.

1   *Make the dressing:* In a small bowl, combine the zest, juice, oil, and salt and mix well with a fork until emulsified.

2   *Make the fennel wedges:* Cut the root ends off the bulbs. Cut each bulb in half lengthwise; remove and discard the tough outer layer. Cut each half lengthwise into 3 wedges about 1 inch (2.5 centimeters) thick, leaving the white core intact so the layers don't fall apart.

3   In a mixing bowl, toss the fennel wedges with the oil, salt, and pepper to taste until they're well coated.

4   The following step can be pretty smoky, so make sure to open a window or turn on the hood vent, if you have one. Heat a wide heavy-bottomed sauté pan over medium-high heat until very hot, about 1 minute. Using kitchen tongs, place the fennel wedges, cut side down, in the pan. Cook until very browned, about 2 minutes. Flip to the other cut side and cook until browned, again about 2 minutes. Turn the wedges onto the curved side and cook for another 2 minutes. They should be softened but still have a bit of crunch. Remove to a bowl or small platter. Drizzle with the dressing, sprinkle with the parsley, and serve.

Serves 4

FOR THE DRESSING:

1 teaspoon grated orange zest

2 tablespoons freshly squeezed orange juice (about ½ an orange)

2 tablespoons extra-virgin olive oil

Pinch of kosher salt

FOR THE FENNEL WEDGES:

3 fennel bulbs (about 2 pounds / 910 grams)

2 tablespoons extra-virgin olive oil

½ teaspoon kosher salt

Freshly ground black pepper

2 tablespoons roughly chopped fresh parsley

STUFFED TOMATOES

Makes 4

4 large beefsteak tomatoes (about 3 pounds / 1.4 kilograms)

1 teaspoon kosher salt, divided

6 tablespoons (90 milliliters) extra-virgin olive oil, divided

½ yellow onion, finely diced

1 clove garlic, pressed or finely minced

4 ounces (115 grams) ground beef

Freshly ground black pepper

2 cups (300 grams) cooked white rice

¼ cup (25 grams) finely chopped fresh dill

Stuffed tomatoes and peppers are a staple in Greek tavernas; they're made in the morning and sit in a heated display case at slightly above room temperature, soaking in their own juices, until they're sold out for the day.

1   Preheat the oven to 375°F (190°C).

2   Using a paring knife, remove circular tops about 3 inches (7.5 centimeters) in diameter from the tomatoes (as on jack-o'-lanterns) and set aside. Using a spoon, scoop out and set aside the insides of each tomato, being careful not to scoop so much out that the tomato will fall apart in the oven. There should be a wall of tomato about ¾ inch (2 centimeters) thick on the sides and slightly thicker on the bottom.

3   Place the tomato pulp in a strainer fitted over a bowl and mash and press with a spoon until you have about ½ cup (120 milliliters) tomato juice in the bowl. Discard the seeds and pulp and set the juice aside.

4   Place the tomatoes, scooped-out sides up, in a baking dish and use ¼ teaspoon of the salt to season the insides.

5   In a wide heavy-bottomed sauté pan, heat 2 tablespoons (30 milliliters) of the oil over medium-high heat for 30 seconds. Add the onion and garlic and cook until the onion is translucent and soft, about 2 minutes.

6   Add the beef, ½ teaspoon of the salt, and pepper to taste and stir well, breaking up the beef with a spoon. Cook until the meat is completely cooked through, 2 to 3 minutes.

7   Add the rice and stir well to combine with the meat and onion.

8   Add the tomato juice and cook, stirring often, until the liquid has been absorbed, 1 to 2 minutes.

9   Remove from the heat, add the dill, and stir to combine. Season generously with more pepper.

10 When the rice mixture is cool enough to handle, spoon about ½ cup (75 grams) of the mixture into each tomato (they should be tightly packed). Replace the tops on the tomatoes. Drizzle with the remaining 4 tablespoons (60 milliliters) oil and rub to make sure the skins are all lightly coated. Sprinkle with the remaining ¼ teaspoon salt.

11 Roast until the exposed rice is lightly browned and the tomatoes are softened but still hold their shape, about 50 minutes. Serve warm or at room temperature.

SAUTÉED SHAVED ASPARAGUS

The increased surface area in these ribbons of asparagus creates a fuller mouthful of flavor with each bite. You will need a mandoline in order to get the translucent, pliable strips of asparagus. It can be a bit tricky, but it's worth the extra time and effort—and once you're done slicing, the actual cooking couldn't be simpler.

1   Use the thickest asparagus you can find so that it will be easier to slice. Snap the woody ends off the asparagus stalks where they break naturally.

2   Using a mandoline, cut the stalks lengthwise into long strips about $\frac{1}{16}$ inch (2 millimeters) thick: Hold the stalk against the mandoline with the palm of your hand or the holder that comes with many brands to protect your fingers. If your mandoline doesn't have one, hold your fingers up to avoid cutting yourself. Starting with the tip, push the stalk through, applying enough pressure to slice easily. Repeat with all the stalks. Note: If you don't have a mandoline, you can use a vegetable peeler.

3   In a large sauté pan, heat the oil over medium heat for 30 seconds.

4   Add the asparagus in a single layer (work in batches if your pan isn't big enough), season with the salt and pepper to taste, and cook, stirring constantly, until tender but still bright green, 2 to 3 minutes.

5   Add the butter and remove from the heat. Stir to coat with the melting butter and serve.

Serves 4

1½ bunches thick asparagus (about 1½ pounds / 680 grams)

1 tablespoon extra-virgin olive oil

½ teaspoon kosher salt

Generous amount of freshly ground black pepper

2 teaspoons good-quality unsalted butter

STRING BEANS

with Fried Shallots, Pecorino & Basil

Serves 4

FOR THE FRIED SHALLOTS:

2 medium shallots, halved and very
thinly sliced

½ cup (120 milliliters) vegetable oil

FOR THE STRING BEANS:

2½ teaspoons kosher salt, divided

1½ pounds (680 grams) string beans,
stem ends trimmed

2 tablespoons extra-virgin olive oil

Freshly ground black pepper

¼ cup (25 grams) finely chopped
fresh basil

2 ounces (55 grams) pecorino cheese,
crumbled

I like the contrast of the dark, charred taste of the string beans and the
fried shallots with the coolness of the basil. Let the string beans cool
completely before mixing them with the other ingredients so that the
flavors remain distinct.

1   *Make the fried shallots:* Place the shallot slices in a single layer on a
    paper towel and press with another paper towel to remove moisture.

2   In a small saucepan, heat the oil over medium-high heat until very hot,
    2 to 3 minutes. Drop in the shallots and fry until golden and crisp, about
    2 minutes. Remove with a slotted spoon and drain on paper towels.

3   Let cool completely. (The shallots will keep for up to 2 months stored
    in an airtight container in a cool, dry place.)

4   *Make the string beans:* In a wide heavy-bottomed sauté pan, bring
    2 inches (5 centimeters) of water and 2 teaspoons of the salt to a boil.

5   Add the beans and cook until they are just tender but still bright green,
    about 6 minutes. Drain and rinse with very cold water to stop them from
    overcooking.

6   Dry the sauté pan and return it to very high heat. Add the oil and
    heat until very hot, 1 to 2 minutes. Add the green beans, the remaining
    ½ teaspoon salt, and a generous amount of pepper. Cook, stirring often,
    until the beans are slightly charred all over, about 3 minutes.

7   Remove from the heat and let cool completely. Combine with the fried
    shallots, basil, and cheese and serve at room temperature.

STRING BEANS

with Lemon & Caramelized Shallots

Serves 4

2½ teaspoons kosher salt, divided

1½ pounds (680 grams) string beans, stem ends trimmed

2 tablespoons extra-virgin olive oil

3 medium shallots, finely minced

3 cloves garlic, pressed or finely minced

1 teaspoon grated lemon zest (from 1 lemon)

Freshly ground black pepper

2 tablespoons freshly squeezed lemon juice (from 1 large lemon)

2 tablespoons roughly chopped fresh parsley

This is one of my favorite dishes in this book, sweet and pungent from the shallots, green and crunchy from the string beans, with a bright finish from the lemon zest and parsley.

1 In a wide heavy-bottomed sauté pan, bring 2 inches (5 centimeters) of water and 2 teaspoons of the salt to a boil.

2 Add the beans and cook until they are just tender but still bright green, about 6 minutes. Drain and rinse with very cold water to stop them from overcooking.

3 Dry the sauté pan and return it to medium-high heat. Add the oil and heat for 30 seconds. Add the shallots and cook until they are completely translucent and beginning to brown, about 2 minutes. Add the garlic and cook until it is softened, about 1 minute.

4 Add the beans, lemon zest, the remaining ½ teaspoon salt, and pepper to taste. Cook, stirring constantly, until the beans are well coated with the shallot-and-garlic mixture and are heated through, about 5 minutes.

5 Add the lemon juice and continue to cook, scraping up browned bits from the bottom of the pan, for about 3 minutes.

6 Remove from the heat, stir in the parsley, and serve.

VEGETABLES IN SPICED BROTH OVER COUSCOUS

I always throw a few carrots and celery stalks into this lightly spiced broth for flavor, but you can substitute with or add to the other vegetables pumpkin, squash, cauliflower, parsnips, or fennel. This recipe is a good way to use up the odd leftover raw vegetables in your fridge. I serve them scooped over heaping bowls of plain couscous for a hearty side dish or vegetarian entrée.

1   In a deep saucepan, heat the butter and oil over medium-high heat until the butter is melted and bubbling, 1 to 2 minutes. Add the onion, ginger, coriander, and cinnamon. Cook, stirring often, until the onion is soft and translucent but not caramelized, 1 to 2 minutes.

2   Add the *harissa* paste and stir to combine. Add 4 cups (960 milliliters) water, the salt, cilantro, and parsley and stir. Bring to a simmer, then add the carrots, turnip, celery, and garbanzo beans and stir to combine. Simmer, uncovered, until the carrots and turnips are just tender but not completely soft, about 10 minutes.

3   Add the zucchini and cook until soft and cooked through, about 5 minutes. Taste the broth for seasoning and add more salt, if desired. You can serve at this point or reduce the heat to a low simmer while you make the rest of your meal.

4   To serve, ladle over a big bowl of the couscous.

Serves 4

2 tablespoons unsalted butter

1 tablespoon extra-virgin olive oil

½ yellow onion, halved and thinly sliced crosswise

½ teaspoon ground ginger

½ teaspoon ground coriander

¼ teaspoon ground cinnamon

1 tablespoon *harissa* paste

2 teaspoons kosher salt, or more to taste

2 sprigs fresh cilantro

2 sprigs fresh parsley

2 carrots (about 8 ounces / 225 grams), peeled and cut into 1-inch (2.5-centimeter) pieces

1 turnip (about 8 ounces / 225 grams), peeled and cut into 1-inch (2.5-centimeter) thick wedges

1 stalk celery, cut into 1-inch (2.5-centimeter) pieces

1 (14-ounce / 400-gram) can garbanzo beans, drained and rinsed

1 zucchini (about 8 ounces / 225 grams), halved lengthwise and cut into 1-inch (2.5-centimeter) pieces

Couscous (page 132)

COUSCOUS

Makes 5 cups (750 grams); serves 4 generously

1 tablespoon extra-virgin olive oil

1 tablespoon unsalted butter

1 teaspoon kosher salt

2 cups (400 grams) couscous

1 In a medium-size saucepan with a tight-fitting lid, combine the oil and butter and cook until the butter is melted.

2 Add 2¼ cups (540 milliliters) water and the salt and bring to a boil.

3 Add the couscous, stir once, cover, and remove from the heat. Let sit for 10 minutes.

4 Uncover and fluff with a fork, separating any lumps, and serve.

The front door of the old **FARMHOUSE** my parents bought in the hills of Kamini (photo taken early '80s)

ZUCCHINI ROUNDS SIMMERED IN FRESH TOMATO SAUCE

Here's another simple but delicious recipe that I stole from my mother. I remember the first time I paid attention to her as she was cooking this dish: I had a kind of slow-motion epiphany when I saw that the secret to the slightly bitter, floral, pungent intensity of the zucchini was a single dried bay leaf. It was an example of the magic of cooking in full force. Just make sure the bay leaf is small or it can tip the whole thing overboard and make the sauce too bitter.

1   In a wide heavy-bottomed sauté pan, heat the oil over medium heat for 30 seconds. Add the garlic and cook, stirring constantly, until the garlic just turns golden around the edges, about 2 minutes.

2   Add the tomatoes, salt, and bay leaf. Cook, stirring often, until the tomatoes are pulpy and broken down, about 5 minutes.

3   Add the zucchini and stir until they are well coated with the tomato sauce. Cover and cook until the zucchini are tender, lifting the lid and stirring occasionally, 6 to 8 minutes.

4   Season generously with pepper and serve.

Serves 4

3 tablespoons (45 milliliters) extra-virgin olive oil

1 clove garlic, thinly sliced

2 ripe vine tomatoes (about 12 ounces / 340 grams), cut into ½-inch (12-millimeter) pieces (seeds and juices included)

½ teaspoon kosher salt

1 small bay leaf

2 zucchini (about 1 pound / 455 grams), cut into ¼-inch (6-millimeter) thick rounds

Freshly ground black pepper

COUSCOUS

with Currants & Pistachios

Serves 4 to 6

1 tablespoon extra-virgin olive oil

1 tablespoon unsalted butter

½ yellow onion, very finely diced

1 teaspoon kosher salt

2 cups (400 grams) couscous

½ cup (76 grams) dried currants

1 cup (240 milliliters) orange juice

½ cup (50 grams) shelled pistachios (or whole raw almonds), finely chopped

¼ cup (15 grams) roughly chopped fresh cilantro

Couscous makes a great accompaniment to saucy braised meats and stews, the tender grainlike semolina pellets soaking up the juices so that you can savor them even longer. While a fluffy bowl of plain couscous cooked with a little butter, oil, and salt works well as a base for more flavorful dishes, this sweet-and-savory version is good enough to eat on its own. The orange-soaked currants add a little dark-fruit intensity, while the pale-green pistachios add a dash of color and meaty heft.

1   In a large saucepan with a tight-fitting lid, combine the oil and butter and cook over medium heat until the butter is melted and bubbling.

2   Add the onion and cook until soft and translucent but not browned, about 3 minutes.

3   Add 2¼ cups (540 milliliters) water and the salt and bring to a boil. Add the couscous, stir once, cover, and remove from the heat. Let sit for 10 minutes.

4   Meanwhile, in a small bowl, soak the currants in the orange juice.

5   Uncover the couscous and fluff with a fork, separating any lumps.

6   Drain the currants and add them to the couscous. Add most of the pistachios and most of the cilantro and mix well to combine. Garnish with the remaining pistachios and cilantro and serve.

DOLMADA PILAF

Dolmades are a popular Greek *mezze*, usually a mixture of rice, ground meat, and fresh herbs wrapped tightly in brined grape leaves and stored in oil. This is basically a deconstructed version; you have all the bold, delicious flavors of the *dolmada* without the time-consuming task of rolling grape-leaf parcels.

1   In a large pan, heat the oil over medium-high heat for 30 seconds. Add the onion and garlic and cook, stirring, until the onion is soft and translucent but not browned, about 3 minutes.

2   Add the beef, salt, and a generous amount of pepper. Cook, stirring, until the meat is completely cooked through, about 3 minutes.

3   Add the rice and stir well to combine. Reduce the heat to low and add the grape leaves, dill, oregano, and lemon juice. Stir well to combine and remove from the heat.

4   Season to taste with more salt and pepper, if desired, and serve.

NOTE: Brined grape leaves can be found near the olives or in the specialty-foods section at the supermarket.

Serves 4

3 tablespoons (45 milliliters) extra-virgin olive oil

1 small yellow onion, finely minced

1 clove garlic, pressed or finely minced

8 ounces (225 grams) ground beef

½ teaspoon kosher salt, or more to taste

Freshly ground black pepper

1 recipe Short-Grain Brown Rice (page 138)

½ cup finely chopped brined grape leaves (see Note)

¼ cup (25 grams) finely chopped fresh dill

1 teaspoon dried oregano

1 tablespoon freshly squeezed lemon juice (from ½ large lemon)

SHORT-GRAIN BROWN RICE

Makes about 2½ cups (375 grams)

1 cup (200 grams) raw short-grain brown rice

1 tablespoon extra-virgin olive oil

¼ teaspoon kosher salt

1   In a saucepan, combine all the ingredients with 2 cups (480 milliliters) water. Bring to a boil, stir once, cover, and reduce the heat to very low. Cook until all the water has been absorbed by the rice, about 50 minutes.

2   Uncover and stir again. Cover and let sit for 10 minutes before serving.

SPRING CENTERPIECE

Use bunches of fresh herbs as a centerpiece; they are a beautiful and inexpensive alternative to flowers, and their scent can complement the flavors of a meal. If you have access to a farmers' market, look for a variety of textures and colors, such as purple basil, chervil, and flowering lavender. Otherwise, you can usually find long-stemmed flat-leaf parsley, bunched rosemary, thyme, and bouquets of mint at your local supermarket. Wash the herbs well under cold running water and shake off excess dampness. This will bring out their scent as well as rinse off any dirt. Fill different-size canning jars, small vases, or clear water glasses halfway with lukewarm water. Trim the root ends off the herbs and place large loose bunches in each jar. Place more delicate herbs, such as thyme and chervil, in smaller jars. If you have a long rectangular table, arrange the jars along the centerline, alternating sizes and types. If you have a smaller round table, cluster them in the center.

STOVETOP SIMMERED POTATOES

This is my version of a simple country-style French side dish. The parsnips infuse the potatoes with their uniquely earthy sweetness.

1 In a wide heavy-bottomed sauté pan, heat the oil over medium-high heat for 30 seconds. Add the onion and cook, stirring often, until soft and beginning to caramelize, about 7 minutes.

2 Add the potatoes and parsnips and stir until they are nicely coated with the onion. Add the stock, bay leaf, and salt.

3 Bring to a boil, cover, and reduce the heat to low. Cook until the potatoes are completely soft, about 15 minutes. Season to taste with pepper and more salt, if desired. Sprinkle with the parsley and serve.

Serves 4

2 tablespoons extra-virgin olive oil

½ yellow onion, thinly sliced

2 red potatoes (about 1 pound / 455 grams), cut into ¼-inch (6-millimeter) thick rounds

2 large parsnips (about 8 ounces / 225 grams), peeled and cut into ¼-inch (6-millimeter) thick rounds

1½ cups (360 milliliters) chicken stock

1 small bay leaf

Heaping ¼ teaspoon kosher salt, or more to taste

Freshly ground black pepper

2 tablespoons roughly chopped fresh parsley

LEMONY ROASTED POTATOES

with Grapes & Rosemary

When I was young there were a few summers when my family ate almost exclusively at a taverna called George & Anna's that overlooked the parked fishing boats in the small port town of Kamini. My sister and I would play in the hulls of abandoned *kaikis,* the Greek word for the painted wooden boats, until the food was ready. Most of the main courses came with a side of delicious lemon-infused boiled potatoes. I always wanted to order an extra plate of them, but George wouldn't let us. You had to savor the allotment of wedges that came with your stuffed tomatoes or lamb chop; the scarcity was part of the appeal. During the day, he would sit on the veranda peeling potatoes for that night's meal, requiring hours of painstaking labor—obviously why he was so proprietary about them.

This recipe is very loosely based on my memory of George's potatoes. I've added the grapes and herbs. The fruit bursts open and caramelizes slightly in the oven, releasing honeylike juices that mingle with the lemon and olive oil, while the parboiling makes the wedges extra crisp.

1 Preheat the oven to 400°F (205°C). Line a baking sheet with foil.

2 Cut the potatoes in half lengthwise. Cut each half lengthwise into wedges 1 inch (2.5 centimeters) thick, about 4 pieces per half. Place the potatoes and 1 teaspoon of the salt in a medium-size pot and cover with cold water.

3 Quarter 1 lemon and squeeze the juice into the pot, then add the lemon rinds to the water. Add the garlic. Bring to a boil and cook for 5 minutes. Drain and discard the lemon and garlic.

4 Place the potatoes on the prepared baking sheet. Add the grapes, drizzle with the oil, sprinkle with the rosemary and the remaining ½ teaspoon salt, season to taste with pepper, and toss to coat.

5 Squeeze the juice of the remaining ½ lemon over the potato-and-grape mixture. Roast until the potatoes are golden and most of the grapes have burst open slightly, about 45 minutes. Serve.

Serves 4

4 Yukon Gold potatoes (about 2 pounds / 910 grams)

1½ teaspoons kosher salt, divided

1½ lemons

2 cloves garlic, halved lengthwise

1 cup (100 grams) seedless red grapes, stems removed

3 tablespoons (45 milliliters) extra-virgin olive oil

1 tablespoon dried rosemary

Freshly ground black pepper

SWEET-POTATO PUREE

Serves 4

3 to 4 sweet potatoes (about 2 pounds / 910 grams)

2½ teaspoons kosher salt, divided, or more to taste

2 tablespoons unsalted butter

2 tablespoons extra-virgin olive oil

Leaves from ½ bunch fresh thyme (about 25 sprigs)

1 yellow onion, diced

Freshly ground black pepper

Thyme is a foolproof herb for roasting meats and vegetables: It's impossible to overdo it, and the scent wafting out of the oven enhances that predinner anticipation of things to come. Here, I tried something a little different by frying fresh thyme leaves in olive oil before mashing them together with cooked sweet potatoes. The woody and aromatic flavor infuses the oil, balancing the candylike sweetness of the potatoes. A nice match for roasted chicken or turkey.

1   Peel the sweet potatoes and cut them into roughly 1-inch (2.5-centimeter) chunks. Place them in a medium-size saucepan and cover with about 2 inches (5 centimeters) of cold water. Add 2 teaspoons of the salt and bring to a boil.

2   Cook until the sweet potatoes are very tender, almost falling apart, about 20 minutes. Drain the potatoes and set aside.

3   Dry and return the pot to medium-high heat and add the butter and oil. Cook until the butter is melted and bubbling, 2 to 3 minutes.

4   Add the thyme leaves; they should sizzle on contact. Cook until crisp, about 3 minutes.

5   Add the onion and cook, stirring occasionally, until soft and translucent, 5 to 7 minutes.

6   Add the sweet potatoes and cook, mashing with a fork or potato masher, until the texture is smooth with no large chunks, the onions are mixed in, and the potatoes are hot.

7   Remove from the heat and season with the remaining ½ teaspoon salt, or more to taste, and a generous amount of pepper. Mix well and serve.

OLIVE OIL MASHED POTATOES

I truly love these rustic mashed potatoes smothered in fruity golden olive oil and laced with salty capers and vibrant dill. The recipe is almost impossible to mess up, since the potatoes are cooked until they're falling apart and everything is simply mashed together with a fork. This is a good dish to serve with roasted or grilled lamb chops.

1   Place the potatoes in a large pot of cold water with 2 teaspoons of the salt and bring to a boil. Cook until the potatoes are very soft and beginning to fall apart, about 20 minutes. Drain well and place the potatoes in a large serving bowl.

2   Add the oil and mash the potatoes with a fork until they are broken down.

3   Add the capers, dill, the remaining ¼ teaspoon salt, or more to taste, and plenty of pepper. Mash until well combined but still slightly chunky. Serve.

Serves 4

4 Yukon Gold potatoes (about 2 pounds / 910 grams), cut into large chunks

2¼ teaspoons kosher salt, divided, or more to taste

¼ cup (60 milliliters) extra-virgin olive oil

2 tablespoons drained capers

2 tablespoons roughly chopped fresh dill

Freshly ground black pepper

There is nothing as purely satisfying as a big bowl of pasta. I find myself craving its uniquely soft, slightly chewy texture and ability to encompass flavors more than any other food. Pasta is also the great fail-safe for hungry people who don't know how to cook. In high school, when I could barely operate the oven, I could still manage to throw together a fairly decent spaghetti puttanesca for myself, if I was desperate.

6

PIZZA & PASTA

My father's entire culinary repertoire consists of dummied-up store-bought pasta sauce (if you don't count his admittedly delicious tuna-salad recipe). Unlike most food, as any lazy college student will tell you, even badly prepared pasta can still be pretty delicious—although a trip to Italy will quickly disabuse you of any notion that your linguine with butter is as good as it can get.

To me, pasta captures the magic of cooking: A rudimentary concoction of flour, eggs, and water becomes the basis for an endless variety of flavors and textures. While fresh pasta is a tender and delicious treat, I rarely find the time to make it at home. I'm slightly ashamed to admit that the pasta-making attachment to my KitchenAid rarely sees the light of day. For this collection of my favorite pasta dishes, I've focused on fresh, simple recipes that you can make with dried penne, spaghetti, fusilli, and farfalle. Based on the pasta specials at the restaurant, these recipes reflect seasonally changing ingredients—juicy snap peas in the spring, intensely flavorful heirloom tomatoes in the summer, honey-sweet butternut squash in the fall, bright lemons and sweet cream in the winter.

The most common mistake with pasta is overcooking; it's easy to absentmindedly wander off and then end up with a colander full of soggy noodles. A babysitter once taught me that the pasta is cooked when you throw it at the wall and it sticks, although I'm not sure if this trick actually works or if it was just a fun excuse to throw spaghetti around the kitchen. It's important for the pasta to maintain its structure so that it can stand up to the other ingredients and give you a fuller, more satisfying bite. It's especially important in these recipes to drain your pasta a minute or two before it feels completely done, because it will continue to cook slightly when it is reheated with the sauce.

In Italy, pasta is lightly dressed in sauce, rather than drowned in it as we're accustomed to in the States. As a child, I liked to keep the sauce separate from my pasta and dole out huge spoonfuls as I ate; the pasta was really just a vehicle for eating a bowlful of Bolognese. Now, I've grown to appreciate the alchemy that occurs when a spicy *arrabiata* sauce clings to the ridges of *penne rigate,* or when spaghetti becomes wrapped in a blanket of luxurious lemony cream.

Pizza shares some of the same magic as pasta, as the simple dough is transformed into a crisp yet chewy conveyor of intense flavor. I use it to serve up unexpected Mediterranean flavors—the pop of sweet-and-acidic pomegranate seeds with pungent goat cheese, tender meaty zucchini with classic melted fresh mozzarella. Served with a big mixed-greens salad and a nice red wine, pastas and pizzas are perfect for a party or a simple dinner.

My husband, FRANKIE, foraging for fresh figs

PENNE ARRABIATA

This simple pasta is definitely in my top five foods of all time. It's incredibly easy to make, with very few ingredients, but the magic of cooking transforms it into something irresistible—tangy, sweet, and mildly spicy. The most important thing is to cook the tomatoes long enough that they reduce into the thick, pulpy sauce you need to really coat the penne.

1 Bring a large pot of salted water to a boil. Add the *penne rigate* and cook until al dente, about 10 minutes. Drain and toss with a little olive oil.

2 Roughly chop the tomatoes, seeds included, into 1-inch (2.5-centimeter) pieces.

3 In a large pot, heat the ¼ cup (60 milliliters) oil over medium heat for 1 minute. Add the tomatoes, garlic, chili flakes, 1 teaspoon salt, and the sugar. Cook, stirring occasionally, until pulpy and very reduced, about 30 minutes. Taste and add more salt, if desired.

4 Add the pasta and cook, stirring, until it is warmed through and completely coated with the sauce. Transfer to a serving bowl.

5 Tear the basil into ½-inch (12-millimeter) pieces and sprinkle over the pasta. Serve immediately.

Serves 4 to 6

Kosher salt

1 pound (455 grams) *penne rigate*

¼ cup (60 milliliters) extra-virgin olive oil, plus more for the pasta

3½ pounds (1.6 kilograms) ripe vine tomatoes (about 8)

3 cloves garlic, pressed or finely minced

1 teaspoon red chili flakes

½ teaspoon sugar

4 fresh basil leaves

FARFALLE WITH FIGS, LEMON & DILL

Serves 4

Kosher salt

1 pound (455 grams) farfalle

¼ cup (60 milliliters) extra-virgin olive oil

6 dried Black Mission figs, stems removed, halved, and thinly sliced crosswise

2 teaspoons grated lemon zest (from 1 to 2 lemons)

2 teaspoons freshly squeezed lemon juice (from ½ small lemon)

Freshly ground black pepper

¼ cup (15 grams) roughly chopped fresh dill

In this pasta, the bright lemon and fresh dill are balanced by the earthy richness of the dried figs. I like to serve this dish at a big meal like Easter dinner because I can prepare it in advance and serve it at room temperature, giving me time to focus on the rest of the cooking. You can substitute Israeli couscous for the pasta for a different consistency.

1   Bring a large pot of salted water to a boil. Add the farfalle and cook until al dente, about 12 minutes. Drain and place in a large serving bowl. Add the oil and toss to coat.

2   Add the figs, zest and juice, ½ teaspoon salt, and a generous amount of pepper. Toss until well combined. Let cool slightly, add the dill, and toss again.

3   Serve at room temperature.

PENNE WITH SUGAR SNAP PEAS & RICOTTA

Sweet, crunchy sugar snaps, mint, and parsley make this pasta taste like a mouthful of spring. I like to make the ricotta myself so that the texture is thick and creamy, although store-bought will work as well. You can make the ricotta on the stovetop while you prepare the rest of the pasta ingredients.

1   Cut the snap peas crosswise on a bias into pieces ¼ inch (6 millimeters) thick. Set aside.

2   Bring a large pot of salted water to a boil. Add the *penne rigate* and cook until al dente, about 10 minutes. Before you drain the pasta, reserve 1 cup (240 milliliters) of the cooking water and set aside. Drain the pasta, place in a large bowl, and toss with a little olive oil.

3   Return the pot to medium-high heat and add the 3 tablespoons (45 milliliters) oil. Heat for 30 seconds, then add the shallots. Cook until softened but not browned, 1 to 2 minutes.

4   Add the snap peas, ¾ teaspoon salt, the chili flakes, and black pepper to taste. Cook, stirring often, until the snap peas are tender but still bright green and slightly crunchy, 3 to 5 minutes.

5   Add the pasta, ricotta, and reserved cooking water to the pot and stir well to combine. Cook until the pasta is warmed through and well coated by the other ingredients. Remove from the heat and let cool slightly. Add most of the mint and parsley and mix well.

6   Transfer to a serving bowl and sprinkle with the remaining herbs and some more black pepper. Serve immediately.

Serves 4

1 pound (455 grams) sugar snap peas, strings removed

Kosher salt

1 pound (455 grams) *penne rigate*

3 tablespoons (45 milliliters) extra-virgin olive oil, plus more for the pasta

2 shallots, halved and thinly sliced crosswise

½ teaspoon red chili flakes

Freshly ground black pepper

1 cup (250 grams) fresh ricotta (see page 54), at room temperature

¼ cup (25 grams) finely chopped fresh mint

¼ cup (25 grams) finely chopped fresh parsley

I don't usually make pizza at home because in New York there is a constant fever-pitched competition over who has the best slice in the city—an ongoing battle of wood-burning ovens versus gas, thin crust versus thick, sauce variations, styles of cheese, and on and on. New Yorkers often have a touchingly fanatical devotion to their favorite spot, so it seems almost against the spirit of things to attempt homemade pizza. Nonetheless, there's something to be said for that straight-out-of-the-oven freshness you only get at home. And these recipes are not so much for classic pizza as for combinations of flavors that I love, using pizza as the vehicle to convey them.

PIZZA PARTY: THREE VARIATIONS

ZUCCHINI PIZZA

The thin layer of zucchini gives this traditional *margherita*-style pizza a bit of fresh-tasting vegetable substance.

1   *Make the sauce:* In a small saucepan, combine all the ingredients and heat over medium-high heat. Bring to a simmer and cook, stirring occasionally, for 2 minutes. Remove from the heat and let cool slightly.

2   *Make the pizza:* Preheat the oven to 500°F (260°C).

3   Let the dough sit out until it is at room temperature. Dust a work surface with flour. Knead the dough in your hands until you've formed a smooth ball. Place the ball on the floured surface, dust lightly with flour, and punch down with your fists. Let sit for 5 minutes and repeat the process, resting for a few minutes between repetitions, until the dough is no longer resistant. Lift up the dough and gently stretch it into a rectangle, rotating it to stretch out all the sides. Place the dough over your fists and gently stretch it until you have a thin rectangle about 10 by 12 inches (25 by 30 centimeters). If the dough is still shrinking back and resisting, let it rest a few minutes and repeat until you have the desired size.

4   Place the dough on a parchment-lined baking sheet.

5   Slice the zucchini as thinly as possible into rounds; use a mandoline if you have one. The slices should be translucent, about 1/16 inch (2 millimeters) thick.

6   Spread the tomato sauce on the pizza dough, leaving 1/2 inch (12 millimeters) bare around the edge.

7   Place the mozzarella slices in a single layer on the pizza (it's okay if the sauce is not completely covered).

8   Layer the zucchini slices over the cheese in an overlapping pattern, leaving no uncovered cheese. Brush the zucchini with the oil and season with a little salt and a generous amount of pepper. Bake until the crust is crisp and golden and the zucchini is cooked through, about 15 minutes.

9   Transfer the pizza to a cutting board. Let cool slightly, then cut into 6 squares.

Makes 6 slices

FOR THE SAUCE:

1 (14-ounce / 400-gram) can crushed tomatoes

1 tablespoon extra-virgin olive oil

2 tablespoons finely chopped fresh basil

1/4 teaspoon kosher salt

1/8 teaspoon sugar

1/8 teaspoon red chili flakes

FOR THE PIZZA:

11 ounces (310 grams) prepared white pizza dough (half of a 22-ounce / 625-gram ball)

1/4 cup (30 grams) all-purpose flour

1 zucchini (about 4 ounces / 115 grams)

4 ounces (115 grams) fresh mozzarella cheese, cut into 1/8-inch (3-millimeter) thick rounds

1 tablespoon extra-virgin olive oil

Kosher salt

Freshly ground black pepper

POMEGRANATE, THYME & GOAT-CHEESE PIZZA

This pizza is as lushly exotic looking as it is unexpectedly delicious. The richly sweet caramelized shallots covered in a snowy blanket of goat cheese and topped with rubylike pomegranate seeds can be served for dinner, for lunch, or as elegant cocktail-party hors d'oeuvres.

Makes 6 slices

11 ounces (310 grams) prepared white pizza dough (half of a 22-ounce / 625-gram ball)

¼ cup (30 grams) all-purpose flour

1 pomegranate

4 tablespoons (60 milliliters) extra-virgin olive oil, divided

1 pound (455 grams) shallots (about 8), halved and thinly sliced

2 tablespoons pomegranate juice

5 ounces (140 grams) aged goat cheese, rind removed, grated

1 tablespoon fresh thyme leaves (from about 6 sprigs)

Freshly ground black pepper

1 Preheat the oven to 500°F (260°C).

2 Let the dough reach room temperature. Dust a work surface with flour. Knead the dough until you've formed a smooth ball. Place the ball on the surface, dust it lightly with flour, and punch down on it with your fists. Let sit for 5 minutes and repeat, resting for a few minutes between repetitions, until the dough is no longer resistant. Lift it up and gently stretch it into a rectangle, rotating it to stretch out all the sides. Place the dough over your fists and gently stretch it to make a thin rectangle about 10 by 12 inches (25 by 30 centimeters). If the dough is still resisting, let it rest a few minutes and repeat until you have the desired size.

3 Place the dough on a parchment-lined baking sheet.

4 Cut the pomegranate in half and reserve one half for another use. Hold the fruit over a bowl and hit it with the back of a wooden spoon to knock the seeds out. Pick out any bits of white membrane that stick to the seeds. You should have about ½ cup (60 grams) seeds.

5 In a wide heavy-bottomed sauté pan, heat 3 tablespoons (45 milliliters) of the oil over medium heat. Add the shallots and cook, stirring, until golden and caramelized, about 10 minutes. Add the pomegranate juice and cook for 1 minute, scraping up the browned bits from the bottom of the pan. Remove from the heat and let cool slightly.

6 Spread the shallots on the pizza dough, leaving ½ inch (12 millimeters) bare around the edge.

7 Top with the cheese. Sprinkle with the pomegranate seeds and thyme. Drizzle with the remaining 1 tablespoon (15 milliliters) oil. Season generously with pepper. Bake until the crust is crisp and golden and the cheese is melted and lightly browned, about 12 minutes.

8 Transfer to a cutting board. Let cool slightly, then cut into 6 squares.

THE OPERA... MAILER

Hedy's Folly

JOAN DIDION

TOMAS TRANSTRÖMER

the g...

THE GREAT FI...

RECOIL

Michael Pollan
and Maira Kalman

FOOD...

NATIONAL BESTSELLER

EA...

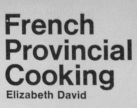

French
Provincial
Cooking

Elizabeth David

ELIZABETH DAVID

IT'S ONLY MAKE

POTATO, FONTINA & TRUFFLE-OIL PIZZA

Makes 6 slices

11 ounces (310 grams) prepared white pizza dough (half of a 22-ounce / 625-gram ball)

¼ cup (30 grams) all-purpose flour

1 Yukon Gold potato (about 4 ounces / 115 grams)

5 ounces (140 grams) Fontina cheese, rind removed, grated

1 tablespoon truffle oil

¼ teaspoon kosher salt

Freshly ground black pepper

In the oven, the rich, musky truffle oil and slightly nutty Italian cheese merge with the paper-thin potatoes into a decadent, golden-crisp pizza.

1   Preheat the oven to 500°F (260°C).

2   Let the dough sit out until it is at room temperature. Dust a work surface with flour. Knead the dough in your hands until you've formed a smooth ball. Place the ball on the floured surface, dust lightly with flour, and punch down with your fists. Let sit for 5 minutes and repeat the process, resting for a few minutes between repetitions, until the dough is no longer resistant. Lift up the dough and gently stretch it into a rectangle, rotating it to stretch out all the sides. Place the dough over your fists and gently stretch it until you have a thin rectangle about 10 by 12 inches (25 by 30 centimeters). If the dough is still shrinking back and resisting, let it rest a few minutes and repeat until you have the desired size.

3   Place the dough on a parchment-lined baking sheet.

4   Slice the potato as thinly as possible into rounds; use a mandoline if you have one. The slices should be translucent, about ¹⁄₁₆ inch (2 millimeters) thick.

5   Sprinkle the cheese on top of the dough, leaving about ½ inch (12 millimeters) bare around the edges.

6   Layer potato slices on top in an overlapping pattern, leaving no uncovered cheese. Drizzle the potatoes with the truffle oil and season with the salt and a generous amount of fresh black pepper.

7   Bake until the crust is crisp and golden and the potatoes are cooked through, about 15 minutes.

8   Transfer the pizza to a cutting board. Let cool slightly, then cut into 6 squares.

SPAGHETTI IN LEMON CREAM

A quintessential Italian dish that is surprisingly easy to make but uniquely delicious. The buttery creaminess is balanced by the equally intense citrus tartness of the lemon. Because the components are so simple, it's important to use the finest ingredients you can find—try to use good-quality cream and fresh lemons for the best results.

1   Bring a large pot of salted water to a boil. Add the spaghetti and cook until al dente, 8 to 10 minutes. Drain and place in a large bowl. Add the oil and toss to coat.

2   Return the pot to medium-high heat and add the cream and ¼ teaspoon salt. Bring to a boil and cook until the cream has thickened and reduced by half, about 3 minutes.

3   Stir in the lemon juice and butter. Bring to a simmer and add the pasta to the pot. Cook, stirring constantly, until all the liquid has been absorbed, 1 to 2 minutes.

4   Divide the pasta among four bowls and season with pepper, if desired. Using a grater or Microplane, shave a generous amount of cheese over each bowl. Tear the basil leaves into roughly ½-inch (12-millimeter) pieces and scatter them over the pasta. Serve immediately.

Serves 4

Kosher salt

1 pound (455 grams) spaghetti

3 tablespoons (45 milliliters) extra-virgin olive oil

1 cup (240 milliliters) heavy cream

½ cup (120 milliliters) freshly squeezed lemon juice (from 4 large lemons)

2 tablespoons unsalted butter

Freshly ground black pepper (optional)

2 ounces (55 grams) Parmesan cheese

16 fresh basil leaves

SPAGHETTI WITH HEIRLOOM CHERRY TOMATOES

Serves 4

Kosher salt

1 pound (455 grams) spaghetti

6 tablespoons (90 milliliters) extra-virgin olive oil, plus more for the pasta

5 cloves garlic, very thinly sliced (use a mandoline if you have one)

2 pints mixed heirloom cherry tomatoes (about 1¼ pounds / 570 grams), cut in half

Freshly ground black pepper

4 ounces (115 grams) fresh mozzarella cheese

12 large fresh basil leaves

Sun-ripe heirloom tomatoes are a part of summer that I look forward to all year. Bursting with natural sweetness, they're best eaten raw or cooked simply to showcase their garden-fresh flavor. This spaghetti with golden garlic, fresh mozzarella, and basil brings out the best in the cherry tomatoes. It can be eaten straight from the stove or served at room temperature for barbecues or picnics.

1   Bring a large pot of salted water to a boil. Add the spaghetti and cook until al dente, 8 to 10 minutes. Drain the pasta, place in a large bowl, and toss with a little oil.

2   Return the pot to the stove. Add the 6 tablespoons (90 milliliters) oil and heat over medium-high heat for 30 seconds. Add the garlic and cook, stirring, until it is soft and some of the edges are just beginning to turn golden, 1 to 2 minutes.

3   Add the tomatoes, ½ teaspoon salt, and pepper to taste. Cook, stirring occasionally, until the tomatoes are juicy and broken down but some still hold their shape, about 5 minutes.

4   Add the pasta to the sauce. Cook, stirring, until well mixed and warmed through, about 1 minute.

5   Remove from the heat and transfer to a large serving bowl, making sure some of the tomato pieces are on top. Let the pasta cool slightly (you don't want the cheese to melt on contact), tear the mozzarella into pieces, and scatter it over the pasta. Do the same with the basil leaves and top with more pepper to taste. Serve immediately.

Winter Pasta:
FUSILLI WITH BUTTERNUT SQUASH

Serves 4

FOR THE FRIED SAGE:

¾ cup (180 milliliters) extra-virgin olive oil

12 fresh sage leaves

FOR THE PASTA:

1 butternut squash (1½ to 2 pounds / 680 to 910 grams)

Kosher salt

1 pound (455 grams) fusilli

3 tablespoons (45 milliliters) extra-virgin olive oil, plus more for the pasta

2 leeks (about ¾ pound / 340 grams), dark green tops removed, halved lengthwise, rinsed well, and thinly sliced

½ teaspoon red chili flakes

1 ounce (30 grams) pecorino cheese, finely grated (about ¼ cup)

At the restaurant, I tend to make variations of popular dishes for the different seasons. In the winter I use sweet, dense butternut squash for this mildly spicy pasta. I like to use fusilli because the shredded squash gets tangled in the little spirals, trapping in the flavor.

1 *Make the fried sage:* In a small frying pan, heat the oil over high heat for 2 minutes. Drop in the sage leaves and fry until they are crisp but still green and stop sizzling, about 45 seconds. Remove the leaves with a slotted spoon and drain on paper towels.

2 *Make the pasta:* Peel the squash, cut it in half, and discard the seeds. Cut the halves into large chunks. Using the grater attachment on a food processor or the large holes on a box grater, shred the squash. Set aside.

3 Bring a large pot of salted water to a boil. Add the fusilli and cook until al dente, about 9 minutes. Before you drain the pasta, reserve 1 cup (240 milliliters) of the cooking water and set aside. Drain the pasta, place in a large bowl, and toss with a little oil.

4 Return the pot to medium-high heat. Add the 3 tablespoons (45 milliliters) oil and heat for 30 seconds. Add the leeks and cook, stirring, until soft but not browned at all, about 4 minutes.

5 Add the squash, 1 teaspoon salt, and the chili flakes and stir well to combine. Add the reserved cooking water and cook until the squash is tender, about 7 minutes.

6 Return the pasta to the pot. Cook, stirring, until it's warmed through and well coated by the other ingredients, about 1 minute.

7 Divide the pasta among four bowls or place in one large serving bowl. Top with the grated cheese and fried sage leaves.

Summer Pasta:

FUSILLI WITH SHREDDED ZUCCHINI

When the weather gets warmer, I opt for summery green zucchini to add sweetness and body to this simple pasta dish.

1   Trim the ends of the zucchini and cut into large chunks. Using the grater attachment on a food processor or the large holes on a box grater, shred the zucchini. Set aside.

2   Bring a large pot of salted water to a boil. Add the fusilli and cook until al dente, about 9 minutes. Before you drain the pasta, reserve 1 cup (240 milliliters) of the cooking water and set aside. Drain the pasta, place in a large bowl, and toss with a little oil.

3   Return the pot to medium-high heat. Add the 3 tablespoons (45 milliliters) oil and heat for 30 seconds. Add the shallots and garlic and cook, stirring, until soft but not browned at all, about 2 minutes.

4   Add the zucchini, chili flakes, ½ teaspoon salt, and black pepper to taste and stir well to combine. Cook until the zucchini is softened, about 3 minutes.

5   Return the pasta to the pot and add the reserved cooking water. Cook until the ingredients are well combined and the pasta is warmed through, about 1 minute.

6   Remove from the heat and stir in the parsley. Divide the pasta among four bowls or place in one large serving bowl. Top with the cheese and serve.

Serves 4

3 zucchini (about 1½ pounds / 680 grams)

Kosher salt

1 pound (455 grams) fusilli

3 tablespoons (45 milliliters) extra-virgin olive oil, plus more for the pasta

2 shallots, cut in half and thinly sliced crosswise

1 clove garlic, pressed or finely minced

½ teaspoon red chili flakes

Freshly ground black pepper

½ cup (30 grams) roughly chopped fresh parsley

1 ounce (30 grams) Parmesan cheese, finely grated (about ¼ cup)

When I was a child, we used to drive out to visit my grandmother in Pennsylvania on the weekends. She lived in a secluded A-frame house set next to a series of small ponds and bordered by the sprawling fields of the surrounding farms. She had been a zoology major in college and was a lifelong outdoorswoman, an avid camper and genuine nature lover. I remember watching her keep a precise calendar tracking the growth stages of a batch of baby snapping turtles that had been born behind her house. She was the kind of woman who could grow her own tomatoes and identify every birdcall.

7
FISH

One weekend when I was about six or seven, my grandmother took my older sister and me to one of the ponds to teach us how to fish. It was clear that we were inveterate city kids with no idea what we were doing. At first I could handle it; waiting peacefully by the water's edge was pleasant, even enjoyable. That all changed as soon as I got a fish on the line. I was completely blindsided by the unexpectedly violent struggle of actually reeling in a fish. At the end of the ordeal, my grandmother cheerfully gutted and cleaned the flounder in front of us, our faces turning pale with shock as the connection between a living fish and the fish we ate dawned on us. That night, my mother pan-fried the fillets for dinner, my sister and I spending the meal shooting each other disgusted looks and poking listlessly at our plates. The experience was a turning point that I still can't get out of my head all these years later; it was the first time I saw what it actually means to eat animals. I didn't turn to vegetarianism, however, and after years of cleaning and breaking down fish in the kitchen, I can now admit that I love eating fish that's as close to its freshly caught state as possible.

For a long time I was wary of cooking with fish. It seemed too delicate an operation, too prone to under- or overcooking. When fish is done badly the result is terrible, but when prepared well it can be a near-perfect experience. It's important to start with a good-quality fresh fish. When I was in the south of France I took endless photographs of the enormous displays of fresh fish in the supermarkets. Whole sardines and black sea bass were packaged daily in those little cellophane-wrapped Styrofoam trays, casually sold as though they were as common as pork chops. Unfortunately, in the United States we don't always have such a wealth of options. When choosing a fish, make sure the eyes are clear and the flesh is firm. If you're cooking with a prepared fillet, it should have a nice bright color and firm flesh as well. Don't be afraid to give it a smell check: Ideally it should smell slightly like seawater (or freshwater if it's a freshwater fish), but not overly fishy. Recently, there has been a growing awareness of the environmentally devastating problem of overfishing, so if at all possible, check the source of your fish for sustainability.

Over the years I've gotten more confident in my fish-cooking abilities, gradually adding more seafood to my repertoire. Most of the recipes that I've included in this chapter are perfectly suited to first-time cooks—such as the almost foolproof grilled sea bass, roasted sardines, and trout. When a recipe is slightly more complicated, I promise the payoff is in the richness of the flavor. Arctic char poached in fragrant olive oil is a revelation, the resulting meat meltingly tender and infused with aromatics. The parchment packaging of the cod can be fussy, but the method creates a fully flavored, hearty dish out of a relatively inexpensive piece of fish.

A KAIKI being pulled in by the captain's daughter

GRILLED MEDITERRANEAN DORADE
with Lemon-Oregano Oil

In my opinion, the greatest thing that Greek food has to offer is perfectly grilled fish. Some of the best meals of my life have been whole grilled fish, both at island tavernas and at my favorite Greek restaurant in Queens. I suspect that there's a special magic to the grills themselves, either through years of use or thanks to the chef's devotion to arcane techniques. At one taverna I know, the proprietor keeps the bed of smoldering coals in his outdoor grill alive by routinely blowing on them with an old electric hair dryer. Even without the lovingly tended grill, this classic preparation of a flaky white Mediterranean fish is a triumph of simplicity. I like to season each bite individually with the lemon oil, freshly ground black pepper, and a tiny pinch of salt.

1   *Make the lemon oil:* In a small bowl, combine all the ingredients and whisk with a fork. Whisk again right before serving.

2   *Make the fish:* Preheat a charcoal or gas grill to medium.

3   Rinse the fish and pat dry. Drizzle with the oil and season both sides with the salt and a generous amount of pepper. Stuff the cavities with the oregano.

4   Place the fish on the grill and cook until nicely blackened, about 7 minutes. Flip and cook until the other side is nicely blackened and the flesh doesn't resist when you press on it, about 7 minutes more.

5   Remove to a serving platter. Bring to the table alongside the bowl of lemon oil, a pepper mill, and salt to season each bite to your taste. This is how I remove the meat from the bones: Cut down the center of the fish straight to the bone (but not through it), then make an angled horizontal cut at the top of the fillet below the head. Gently flip open the fish, as if opening a book; the top fillet should come off smoothly if the meat is cooked through. Lift out the skeleton and head and discard, leaving the other fillet ready to eat as well.

NOTE: If *dorade* is unavailable, you can substitute any whole Mediterranean whitefish, such as red snapper, branzino, or porgy.

Serves 4, or 2 very hungry people

FOR THE LEMON OIL:

¼ cup (60 milliliters) freshly squeezed lemon juice (from 2 large lemons)

¼ cup (60 milliliters) extra-virgin olive oil

¼ teaspoon kosher salt

1 teaspoon dried oregano

FOR THE FISH:

2 (¾- to 1-pound / 340- to 455-gram) whole *dorade* (also called Mediterranean sea bass), gutted and scaled (see Note)

2 tablespoons extra-virgin olive oil

1 teaspoon kosher salt, plus more for serving

Freshly ground black pepper

1 small bunch fresh oregano

Saffron
FISH STEW

Serves 4

FOR THE BROTH:

1 leek

6 cups (1.4 liters) fish stock

1 cup (240 milliliters) clam juice

Grated zest of 1 large orange

Juice of 1 large orange

1 carrot, peeled and roughly chopped

3 cloves garlic

A few sprigs fresh parsley

A few sprigs fresh thyme

1 bay leaf

¼ teaspoon crumbled saffron

FOR THE STEW:

2 large leeks

2 tablespoons unsalted butter

8 ounces (225 grams) carrots (4 medium carrots), peeled and cut into ½-inch (12-millimeter) rounds

8 ounces (225 grams) cauliflower, cut into 1-inch (2.5-centimeter) florets (about ½ a head of cauliflower)

1 pound (455 grams) skinless halibut fillet, cut into 1-inch (2.5-centimeter) pieces

8 ounces (225 grams) squid, bodies cut into ½-inch (12-millimeter) rounds

4 ounces (115 grams) medium shrimp, shelled and deveined

½ teaspoon kosher salt

Freshly ground black pepper

8 ounces (225 grams) mussels, scrubbed and debearded

¼ cup (15 grams) roughly chopped fresh cilantro

¼ cup (15 grams) roughly chopped fresh parsley

This stew is loosely modeled on a traditional Provençal bouillabaisse.

1   *Make the broth:* Remove the darkest green top of the leek and trim the root end. Cut in half lengthwise and rinse well under cold running water, peeling back the layers to remove any dirt. Combine the leek and all the remaining broth ingredients in a stockpot, bring to a boil, and cook until reduced by approximately a third, about 25 minutes. Remove from the heat and strain into another pot. Discard the solids.

2   *Make the stew:* Remove the darkest green top and trim the root end of each leek. Cut each leek in half lengthwise and rinse well under cold running water, peeling back the layers to remove any dirt. Cut crosswise into ½-inch (12-millimeter) pieces.

3   Add the leeks, butter, and carrots to the broth and bring to a boil over medium-high heat. Cook until the carrots are just tender, about 5 minutes.

4   Add the cauliflower and cook until just tender, about 5 minutes.

5   While the vegetables are cooking, in a large bowl, combine the fish, squid, and shrimp and season with the salt and a few turns of pepper.

6   Reduce the heat to a simmer and add the fish, squid, and shrimp to the pot. Add the mussels, cover, and cook until the mussels are open and the fish is cooked through, about 5 minutes.

7   Remove from the heat. Taste for seasoning and add more salt, if desired. Ladle the stew into bowls and sprinkle with the cilantro and parsley.

OLIVE OIL-POACHED ARCTIC CHAR

with Spring Mushrooms & Peas

Serves 4

FOR THE PEAS AND MUSHROOMS:

Kosher salt

2 cups (400 grams) shelled English peas
(you can substitute frozen peas)

4 ounces (115 grams) shiitake
mushrooms

4 ounces (115 grams) chanterelle
mushrooms

2 tablespoons extra-virgin olive oil

½ tablespoon unsalted butter

2 shallots, halved and thinly sliced
crosswise

Freshly ground black pepper

2 teaspoons rice vinegar

This dish is a combination of delicate flavors—nothing too big, bold, or overwhelming: earthy mushrooms, the mild meatiness of the arctic char, and a springlike green sweetness from the fresh English peas. Gently poaching the fish in an aromatic olive oil yields an extremely tender fillet lightly infused with garlic, thyme, and lemon. If I'm in the mood for something much simpler, I'll serve the poached fish over a bed of frisée that has been lightly dressed with lemon and olive oil.

1   *Make the peas and mushrooms:* Bring a pot of well-salted water to a boil. Add the peas and cook until they float to the top and are tender, 2 to 3 minutes. Drain and rinse with cold water.

2   Remove and discard the stems of the shiitakes (or reserve them for another use, such as enriching a stock). Slice the caps very thinly crosswise.

3   Trim off and discard the ends of the chanterelle stems. Quarter the chanterelles lengthwise.

4   In a sauté pan, heat the oil and butter over medium-high heat until the butter is melted and bubbling, about 30 seconds. Add the shallots and cook until soft but not browned, about 2 minutes.

5   Add the mushrooms, season with a heaping ¼ teaspoon salt and pepper to taste, and cook until the mushrooms are softened, about 2 minutes.

6   Add the vinegar and cook until the liquid has been absorbed, about 30 seconds.

7   Add the peas and cook until warmed through, about 30 seconds. Remove from the heat and set aside.

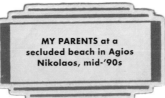

MY PARENTS at a secluded beach in Agios Nikolaos, mid-'90s

8 *Make the fish:* Season both sides of the fish, using ¼ teaspoon salt per fillet and pepper to taste.

9 Place 2 cups (480 milliliters) oil in a deep sauté pan wide enough to accommodate all of the fillets. You should have about 1½ to 2 inches (4 to 5 centimeters) of oil; add more if necessary. Add the thyme, lemon, garlic, and bay leaf. Heat over very low heat until the oil is as warm as a very hot bath. A few small bubbles should be forming on the sides of the pan but the garlic and lemon shouldn't be sizzling.

10 Place the fillets in the pan so that they are just covered by the oil. Poach until just cooked through, about 5 minutes.

11 Arrange the pea-and-mushroom mixture on a platter, or on four plates for individual portions. Transfer the fish with a slotted spoon and place on top of the mixture. Garnish with pea shoots and serve.

FOR THE FISH:

4 (8-ounce / 225-gram) arctic char fillets, about 1½ inches (4 centimeters) thick, skinned (you can substitute salmon)

1 teaspoon kosher salt

Freshly ground black pepper

2 cups (480 milliliters) extra-virgin olive oil, or more as needed

3 sprigs fresh thyme

½ lemon, cut into quarters

2 cloves garlic

1 bay leaf

1 cup (30 grams) spring-pea shoots (you can substitute watercress)

ROASTED BROOK TROUT

with Fennel Seeds

I had a version of this dish at a small family-run restaurant called Chez Thom outside Aix-en-Provence. I was completely blown away by the strong flavor of such a deceptively simple preparation. The toasted fennel seeds infuse the meaty fish with both anise- and nutlike aromas.

1 Preheat the oven to 450°F (230°C). Line a baking sheet with parchment paper.

2 Place the fennel seeds in a dry frying pan over high heat and cook, stirring constantly, until golden and fragrant, about 2 minutes. Remove to a plate.

3 Place the trout on the prepared baking sheet. Drizzle the inside and both outer sides of each fish with the oil. Season with a heaping ½ teaspoon salt per fish and plenty of pepper.

4 Sprinkle the inside of each fish with ½ teaspoon fennel seeds and close up the fish. Sprinkle the top of each fish with ¼ teaspoon fennel seeds.

5 Roast until the skin is crisp and slightly golden on the outside and the meat is cooked through, about 15 minutes.

Serves 4

3 teaspoons fennel seeds

4 (10-ounce / 280-gram) whole brook trout, deboned from the belly but kept whole with the head on

¼ cup (60 milliliters) extra-virgin olive oil

2½ teaspoons kosher salt

Freshly ground black pepper

ROASTED SARDINES

with Grape *Gremolata*

Serves 4

FOR THE GRAPE *GREMOLATA*:

½ cup (50 grams) seedless red grapes

½ cup (30 grams) roughly chopped
  fresh parsley

1 clove garlic, pressed or finely minced

1 teaspoon lemon zest (from 1 lemon)

¼ cup (60 milliliters) extra-virgin
  olive oil

½ teaspoon kosher salt

FOR THE SARDINES:

8 whole good-sized fresh sardines,
  gutted and scaled

3 tablespoons (45 milliliters)
  extra-virgin olive oil

1 teaspoon kosher salt

Freshly ground black pepper

I was inspired to experiment with sardine recipes by my sister's romantic description of a near-perfect meal she had at a seaside café in Essaouira, Morocco: grilled sardines, a wedge of lemon, and an orange soda. My version is roasted, the salty dark meat of the fish balanced by the lush sweetness of the grapes and a hint of lemon zest. Visually, I love the way the crisped silver skin looks against the bright purples and greens of the *gremolata*.

1 *Make the grape gremolata:* Quarter the grapes lengthwise and place them in a small mixing bowl. Add the parsley, garlic, lemon zest, oil, and salt and mix well to combine. (You can prepare the *gremolata* in advance and store, covered, in the refrigerator for up to 3 days. Make sure to let it come to room temperature and stir before use.)

2 *Make the sardines:* Preheat the oven to 400°F (205°C).

3 Rinse the sardines and pat them dry with paper towels.

4 Line a baking sheet with aluminum foil and place the sardines on top. Drizzle with the oil and toss to coat. Season both sides with the salt and a generous amount of pepper.

5 Roast until the skin of the sardines is slightly browned and the meat comes off the bone easily, 10 to 15 minutes, depending on the size of your sardines.

6 Using a fish spatula, gently remove to a platter. Spoon the *gremolata* over the sardines and serve.

PARCHMENT-STEAMED COD

with Olive-Orange *Gremolata*

Serves 4

FOR THE ORANGE BUTTER:

¼ cup (½ stick / 50 grams) unsalted butter, very soft

1 teaspoon grated orange zest (from 1 large orange)

FOR THE *GREMOLATA*:

1 orange

½ cup (90 grams) pitted kalamata olives, roughly chopped

½ cup (30 grams) roughly chopped fresh parsley

¼ cup (60 milliliters) extra-virgin olive oil

1 clove garlic, pressed or finely minced

FOR THE FISH:

4 leeks

2 tablespoons extra-virgin olive oil

1¼ teaspoons kosher salt, divided

4 (6-ounce / 170-gram) skinless cod fillets

Freshly ground black pepper

4 teaspoons dry vermouth

1 large egg, lightly beaten

4 (16-by-13-inch / 40.5-by-33-centimeter) rectangles of parchment paper (see Note)

This is one of the first dishes I developed for the dinner menu at The Smile. We didn't have a grill, gas ovens, or any ventilation, so I came up with this parchment-cooked cod so that the whole restaurant wouldn't smell like cooking fish. While it's a little finicky, I love this method because the ingredients all steam together, infusing the cod with lots of flavor. It's also great to make for dinner parties, since you can prepare the parchment packets in advance, keep them in the fridge, and throw them in the oven about fifteen minutes before you're ready to eat.

1   *Make the orange butter:* In a small bowl, combine the butter and orange zest and mix until well combined. Refrigerate until ready to use.

2   *Make the gremolata:* Cut off both ends of the orange. Using a paring knife, follow the curve of the fruit to cut off the peel and white pith. Working over a bowl to catch the juices, cut out the fruit segments from the membrane and place them in the bowl; squeeze the juice out of the membrane and discard. Roughly chop the orange segments and return them to the bowl. Add the olives, parsley, oil, and garlic and mix well.

3   *Make the fish:* Preheat the oven to 400°F (205°C).

4   Remove the darkest green top and the root end of each leek. Cut each leek in half lengthwise and rinse well under cold running water, peeling back the layers to remove any dirt. Slice crosswise very thinly.

5   In a sauté pan, heat the oil over medium-high heat for 30 seconds. Add the leeks and season with ¼ teaspoon of the salt. Cook until the leeks are softened but not browned, about 8 minutes. Remove from the heat and let cool slightly.

6   Season the cod fillets with ¼ teaspoon salt each and pepper to taste.

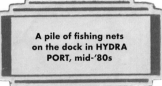

A pile of fishing nets on the dock in HYDRA PORT, mid-'80s

7   Fold one piece of parchment in half from left to right like a book, press to crease, and unfold again. Place one-quarter of the cooked leeks in a mound in the right half of the parchment, slightly off center, closer to the crease. Place one cod fillet on top of the leeks. Top with 1 tablespoon of the orange butter. Spread ¼ cup of the *gremolata* on top and splash with 1 teaspoon of the vermouth.

8   Brush the entire edge of the parchment with the egg. Fold the parchment closed over the fish. Starting at the top left corner, using your fingers, fold the edge over and crease tightly, then repeat, following the edge of the parchment, folding and creasing so that you have a tightly closed half circle. Repeat the procedure with the remaining fillets.

9   Place the parchment packets on a baking sheet. (At this point they can be refrigerated until you're ready to cook them.) Bake for 15 minutes. The parchment should puff up in the oven. Serve in the packets and tear them open at the table.

NOTE: You can sometimes find precut rectangles of parchment paper at the supermarket; otherwise cut them from a roll.

When it comes to cooking meat, one of the most important methods to master is browning. The essence of good meat flavor comes from that deliciously sweet "roastiness." At cooking school, my extremely formal chef instructors taught me that the French word for the brown bits that form in the bottom of your cooking pan is *sucs* (from the word *sucre*, meaning "sugar"). I find myself mumbling that word under my breath as I'm cooking, watching a piece of meat sizzle, the edges turning golden and crisp. Those deposits of caramelized protein are the source of the rich, dark taste we associate with meat-based stews and sauces.

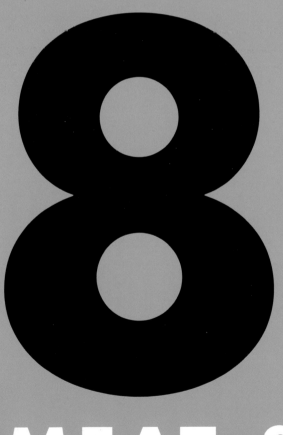

8

MEAT & POULTRY

In my opinion, one of the most detrimental inventions for the kitchen has been the nonstick pan. Admittedly there are some uses for it, but for the most part it has set home cooks back—a triumph of supposed ease over quality. When I first moved out of my parents' house and had to stock my tiny kitchen from scratch, *sucs* were the last thing on my mind. I went for the cheapest nonstick pan because it seemed like the most versatile and convenient choice. I've come a long way since then; I've realized you need only a few basic items to cook well as long as you make informed choices, and that unless you're cooking eggs, baking a cake, or searing a tricky piece of fish, it's best to stay away from Teflon. The same coating that prevents your meat from sticking prevents you from getting a good sear and weakens the ultimate flavor of the dish. I recommend using cast iron, especially enamel-coated cast iron, for browning meat. With common sense and regular care, a quality piece of cookware—unlike my long-gone nonstick pan—can quite easily last a lifetime. If you don't have cast iron, any wide heavy-bottomed metal pan will do.

When you're searing meat, don't rush yourself or be too timid. Make sure to let your pan get nice and hot, and cook the meat in batches if necessary so you don't overcrowd the pan and cause the meat to steam. There should be enough room for some air to circulate around each piece. Finally, don't force the meat with your kitchen tongs. Let it sit untouched until it releases easily from the pan, which means it's ready.

I'm going on and on about browning because as I was testing and retesting all of these recipes, I started to see that the early mistake of not browning correctly is one of the major ways that you can go wrong. You'll end up with a dish that doesn't have the depth or flavor that it should have. The braised lamb shank definitely needs a good sear to melt off some of the rich fat and to create a base note for the sweet and tangy broth. In the sauce for the sliced flank steak, the delicately flavored mushrooms need the meaty jolt from being cooked in the same pan as the steak. If you get a crisp, dark golden sear on the chicken, it will impart a meaty heft to your puttanesca sauce.

Most people treat meat as the main event of any meal. While I love vegetables, there's something to be said for a hearty and intensely flavorful cornerstone dish at dinner. That doesn't mean you have to eat huge portions of red meat to be satisfied (the occasional grilled steak notwithstanding); on the contrary, I think of meat and poultry as elements you can add sparingly to each bite, savoring the unique texture and taste. Still, there's a satisfying drama in bringing a whole piece of meat to the table—an aromatic herb-rubbed lamb leg on a cutting board, an elegantly blackened roast turkey arranged on a simple bed of orange slices, or a Dutch oven bubbling with fragrant spiced tomato sauce and cinnamon-scented lamb meatballs.

LAMB SHANKS
with Dates & Preserved Lemon

I based this dish on a very hearty lunch I once had in Marseille. I was starving after hours of wandering around the bustling port town, scouring its many open-air markets and spice shops. I came across an old Tunisian café decorated with beautiful floor-to-ceiling blue and white tiles and bowls of bright red house-made *harissa* on each table. When my lamb shank arrived, I loved the drama and simplicity of being served a big piece of meat melting off the bone, as well as the sweet-and-savory richness of the broth. This dish goes very well with a big bowl of plain couscous (see page 132) to soak up the broth.

1   Season the lamb on both sides with the salt and a generous amount of black pepper. In a large heavy-bottomed pot or Dutch oven, heat the oil over medium-high heat for about 2 minutes. Brown the shanks on all sides, working in batches if necessary, until lightly golden (about 5 minutes per batch). Remove the shanks from the pot and set aside on a plate.

2   Reduce the heat to medium. Add the onion, garlic, coriander, cinnamon, and cayenne and cook, stirring, until the onion is soft and translucent, about 4 minutes.

3   Add the carrots and ginger and cook, stirring, until the onion begins to caramelize, about 3 minutes.

4   Add the dates and preserved lemon and stir to combine. Add the tomatoes and stock and stir to combine. Return the lamb and any meat juices to the pot; the lamb should be just covered with liquid (if needed, add a little more stock).

5   Partially cover the pot by placing the lid slightly askew so some steam can escape and bring the liquid to a boil. Reduce the heat to a simmer and cook until the lamb is tender and falling off the bone, at least 1 hour and 15 minutes.

6   Place the yogurt in a small bowl and the cilantro sprigs in another. Serve alongside the lamb so everyone can garnish as they like.

NOTE: If you don't feel like dealing with shanks, you can make this recipe as a stew by substituting 2½ pounds boneless lamb shoulder or leg cut into 2-inch pieces.

Serves 4

4 lamb shanks on the bone (4 to 5 pounds / 1.8 to 2.3 kilograms) (see Note)

2 teaspoons kosher salt

Freshly ground black pepper

3 tablespoons (45 milliliters) extra-virgin olive oil

1 yellow onion, halved and thinly sliced

3 cloves garlic, pressed or finely minced

½ teaspoon ground coriander

¼ teaspoon ground cinnamon

⅛ teaspoon cayenne pepper

3 carrots, peeled and cut into 1-inch (2.5-centimeter) chunks

1 tablespoon minced fresh ginger

8 dates, pitted and halved lengthwise

2 halves preserved lemon (see page 36)

1 (14-ounce / 400-gram) can diced tomatoes, with their juice

4 cups (960 milliliters) chicken stock, or more if necessary

1 cup (250 grams) plain Greek yogurt

1 small bunch cilantro sprigs

MINTED LAMB ROAST

Serves 6

½ cup (50 grams) finely chopped fresh mint (from 1 large bunch)

¼ cup (60 milliliters) extra-virgin olive oil

2 tablespoons grated orange zest (from about 4 oranges)

2 shallots, finely minced

1 (3½-pound / 1.6-kilogram) boneless leg of lamb, at room temperature

1½ teaspoons kosher salt, divided

Freshly ground black pepper

For this roast I was inspired by the use of mint and orange in a recipe for Persian lamb stew in one of my favorite cookbooks, Diana Henry's *Crazy Water Pickled Lemons*. I find that one of the easiest ways to get a good jolt of flavor on a boned lamb leg roast is to rub it with a concentrated mixture inside and out. The minced shallots melt as the leg roasts, while the mint and orange seep into the tender lamb meat.

1   Preheat the oven to 375°F (190°C).

2   In a small bowl, combine the mint, oil, orange zest, and shallots. Mix well.

3   Unroll the lamb leg and rub half the mixture into the inside. Season with ½ teaspoon of the salt and a generous amount of pepper. Roll up the leg and tie it tightly with butcher twine every 2 inches to hold the roast together.

4   Rub the rest of the mint mixture on the outside of the lamb and season with the remaining 1 teaspoon salt and a generous amount of pepper.

5   Place the lamb on a baking sheet and cook until a thermometer inserted into the deepest part of the meat reads 130°F (55°C) for rare, about 50 minutes.

6   Let rest for at least 5 minutes, then slice thinly against the grain and serve.

MOROCCAN MEATBALLS

The scent of cinnamon and lamb cooking together reminds me of a Marrakech market stall at night. These meatballs have become something of a standby both in my home kitchen and at the restaurant. The unexpected warmth of the cinnamon and spices has been a big hit with customers and friends, and if there are any leftovers at the end of the dinner shift, the waitstaff eagerly scoops them up for a late-night snack. It's a great dish to make for large parties—I like to have a heaping pot simmering on the stove and serve it with lots of warm bread to mop up the flavorful tomato sauce.

1   Preheat the oven to 400°F (205°C). Line a baking sheet with aluminum foil or parchment paper.

2   Heat a pan over medium-high heat. Add 1 tablespoon oil. Add the onions and cook, stirring, until soft but not browned, about 5 to 7 minutes. Let cool slightly.

3   In a large bowl, combine the lamb, bread crumbs, eggs, cooked onion, parsley, cinnamon, salt, and a generous amount of pepper. Mix with your hands until well combined.

4   Roll the lamb mixture into 1½-inch (4-centimeter) balls (about the size of ping-pong balls) and arrange in rows on the prepared baking sheet.

5   Bake for 10 minutes. The meatballs should be cooked through and slightly browned.

6   Meanwhile, in a heavy-bottomed pot, combine the tomatoes, the remaining 1 tablespoon oil, *ras el hanout*, and a little more than half of the chopped cilantro (reserve the rest for garnish) and place over medium heat. Bring to a simmer and cook, stirring occasionally, until the tomato loses its raw taste and the flavors are well combined, at least 15 minutes.

7   Add the meatballs and about 1 tablespoon of the fat from the baking sheet to the tomato sauce and stir well. Cover and cook for at least 10 minutes over medium-low heat. The meatballs can sit in the sauce over low heat for as long as you like; just make sure to stir them occasionally and keep the heat low so that they won't stick to the bottom of the pot. Serve hot, garnishing with the remaining cilantro.

Serves 4

2 tablespoons extra-virgin olive oil, divided

¾ cup (100 grams) finely minced yellow onion

1½ pounds (680 grams) ground lamb

1½ cups (150 grams) bread crumbs

2 large eggs

¼ cup (25 grams) packed finely chopped fresh parsley

2 teaspoons ground cinnamon

1½ teaspoons kosher salt

Freshly ground black pepper

1 (28-ounce / 840-gram) can crushed tomatoes

½ teaspoon *ras el hanout*, or ¼ teaspoon ground cumin and ¼ teaspoon ground coriander

½ cup (30 grams) roughly chopped fresh cilantro, divided

PEPPERY GRILLED RIB EYE

with Charred Scallions

Serves 4

4 (1½-pound / 680-gram) bone-in rib-eye steaks, 1½ inches (4 centimeters) thick

4¼ teaspoons kosher salt, divided

2 tablespoons coarsely ground mixed red, white, black, and green peppercorns

2 bunches scallions

2 tablespoons extra-virgin olive oil

A really good steak is best prepared in the simplest way possible. I'd much rather cook at home and spend money on a quality cut of meat than go out and spend it on the restaurant markup. My secret, if you can call it that, is to use lots of coarsely ground red, white, green, and black pepper. Other than that, it's nothing but steak and salt. In the winter I cook my rib eyes in a cast-iron skillet over high heat; it works wonderfully, except that the kitchen fills up with smoke, and while you get a nice crisp sear, you don't get that unique char-grilled flavor.

I hate the lingering aftertaste of raw scallions, but when blackened on the grill they take on a delicious, intense sweetness that pairs nicely with a bite of perfectly cooked steak.

1   Let the steaks sit out until they come to room temperature; this will help them cook more evenly and get a good sear.

2   Season each steak with ½ teaspoon of the salt and ¾ teaspoon of the ground peppercorns per side.

3   Trim the root ends of the scallions very slightly so they still hold together. Rinse and dry the scallions and toss them with the oil and the remaining ¼ teaspoon salt.

4   Preheat a charcoal or gas grill to high heat.

5   Place the steaks in the center of the grill and arrange the scallions around the outside of the steaks for less direct heat. Cook the steaks for 7 minutes, until nicely seared, then flip and cook for another 7 minutes for medium-rare. Remove to a platter and let rest for 5 minutes.

6   Cook the scallions, turning once, until soft and nicely charred, for about the same length of time as the steaks, depending on the heat of your grill. You can serve the scallions alongside the steaks or arrange them on top.

PORK & CRANBERRY BEANS

with Rosemary Butter

To me, rosemary is the herb—distinctive and fragrant—that captures the essence of Greek and Italian cooking. I tend to think you can never have enough of it. In this dish the sweet, intensely herbal rosemary butter takes the lead, complementing the light nuttiness of the cranberry beans and darker, milky flavor of the pork sirloin. Raw fresh cranberry beans have a beautiful white-and-crimson splatter pattern but turn a lovely pale violet when cooked.

1   *Marinate the pork:* Place the cutlets in a bowl and add the buttermilk, rosemary, garlic, and Tabasco sauce, turning to coat. Place the bowl in the refrigerator and marinate for at least 1 hour. Bring the pork to room temperature before cooking.

2   *Meanwhile, make the rosemary butter:* In a small saucepan, cook the butter over very low heat until completely melted. Scoop off and discard the white foamy substance that rises to the top. Add the rosemary, increase the heat to medium, and cook for 1 minute. Remove from the heat and let cool. Remove and discard the rosemary sprigs.

3   *Make the cranberry beans:* Place the cranberry beans in a medium pot and cover with cold water. Add the salt and bay leaf and bring to a boil. Cook until tender, about 15 minutes. Drain and toss with 1 tablespoon of the rosemary butter, season to taste with pepper, and cover to keep warm.

4   *Cook the pork:* Remove the cutlets from the marinade and season both sides with the salt (about ½ teaspoon for each cutlet) and a generous amount of pepper. In a sauté pan, heat 2 tablespoons of the rosemary butter over medium-high heat. Add the cutlets and cook until golden, about 3 minutes; drizzle the tops of the cutlets with 1 tablespoon rosemary butter while they're cooking. Flip the cutlets and cook until golden on the second side, about 3 minutes.

5   Remove the cutlets to a platter and scatter the beans on top. Garnish with parsley, if desired, and serve.

Serves 4

FOR THE PORK:

4 (8-ounce / 225-gram) pork cutlets (also called pork sirloin), ½ inch (12 millimeters) thick

2 cups (480 milliliters) buttermilk

2 sprigs fresh rosemary

2 cloves garlic, halved

1 teaspoon Tabasco sauce

2 teaspoons kosher salt

Freshly ground black pepper

2 tablespoons roughly chopped fresh parsley (optional)

FOR THE ROSEMARY BUTTER:

6 tablespoons (¾ stick / 80 grams) unsalted butter

1 (¾-ounce / 20-gram) container fresh rosemary sprigs, or 1 small bunch

FOR THE CRANBERRY BEANS:

1 pound (455 grams) fresh cranberry beans in pods, shelled (about 2 cups)

2 teaspoons kosher salt

1 bay leaf

Freshly ground black pepper

ROSEMARY & OREGANO PORK CHOPS

Serves 4

¼ cup (25 grams) finely chopped fresh rosemary (from 1 small bunch)

¼ cup (25 grams) finely chopped fresh oregano (from 1 small bunch)

2 cloves garlic, pressed or finely minced

¼ cup plus 2 tablespoons (90 milliliters) extra-virgin olive oil, divided

4 bone-in pork rib chops, 1 inch (2.5 centimeters) thick

2 heaping teaspoons kosher salt, divided

Freshly ground black pepper

2 lemons, cut in half crosswise

This is my version of a bright, summery pork chop with lots of rich herb flavor. The recipe is good for lamb chops as well—just reduce the cooking time a bit. I like to add the lemon halves to the roasting pan so that they soften and warm just a bit in the oven, making it easier to squeeze them over the finished chops.

1   Preheat the oven to 400°F (205°C). Line a baking sheet with aluminum foil.

2   In a small bowl, combine the rosemary, oregano, garlic, and ¼ cup (60 milliliters) of the oil and mix well. Rub the mixture over both sides of each pork chop. (At this point you can set the chops aside to marinate while you prepare the rest of your meal, or marinate them in the refrigerator overnight. Bring them to room temperature before continuing with the recipe.)

3   Season both sides of the chops with salt (a heaping ¼ teaspoon per side) and a generous amount of pepper.

4   In a heavy-bottomed frying pan, preferably cast iron, heat the remaining 2 tablespoons (30 milliliters) oil over medium-high heat until very hot, 1 to 2 minutes.

5   Place the pork chops in the pan and cook until golden and crisp, about 3 minutes, then flip and cook the other side for about 3 minutes. If all the chops won't fit in your pan, work in batches.

6   Place the seared chops on the prepared baking sheet. Arrange the lemon halves around the chops and bake for 10 minutes. They should be just cooked through but still juicy and slightly pink. Let the chops rest for a few minutes.

7   Serve with the cooked lemon halves and squeeze them over the pork chops at the table.

VEAL STEW

with Melted Leeks & Braised Radishes

Serves 4

1 tablespoon all-purpose flour

¼ teaspoon ground white pepper

2½ pounds (1.2 kilograms) boneless veal stew meat, cut into 1½-inch (4-centimeter) pieces

1 teaspoon kosher salt

Freshly ground black pepper

2 tablespoons plus 2 teaspoons unsalted butter, divided

2 large leeks (about 1 pound / 455 grams), dark green tops removed, halved lengthwise, cleaned, and thinly sliced

2 cloves garlic, very thinly sliced

2 tablespoons fresh thyme leaves

4 cups (960 milliliters) chicken stock

8 large red radishes, ends trimmed, quartered lengthwise

2 tablespoons plain Greek yogurt or buttermilk

2 tablespoons roughly chopped fresh parsley

I think veal is making a slow but steady comeback in the United States, after horror stories about the industry's mistreatment of calves surfaced in the 1980s. I've noticed a growing number of producers and small farms making a commitment to humane practices and an increased availability of free-range pink or rose veal. Personally, I hope this trend continues, because I love cooking with this tender meat. Its low fat content and subtle flavor make it perfect for slow braising, which prevents it from becoming tough and allows time for the meat to absorb the aromas of the other ingredients. This stew is one of my favorite hearty winter meals, a nod to the classic French cooking I learned in culinary school, with the addition of pale leeks and lovely bright radishes that I saw in the markets in Provence.

1   In a small bowl, combine the flour and white pepper and stir. In a medium bowl, toss the veal with the flour mixture until well coated. Season with the salt and black pepper to taste.

2   In a large heavy-bottomed stockpot or Dutch oven, heat 2 tablespoons of the butter over medium-high heat until melted and bubbling, 1 to 2 minutes. Add the veal and brown on all sides, about 5 minutes; do this in batches if necessary. Return the veal to the bowl and set aside.

3   Add the remaining 2 teaspoons butter to the pot and let it melt. Add the leeks and garlic. Cook, stirring and scraping up the browned bits from the bottom of the pot, until soft, about 3 minutes.

4   Return the veal to the pot along with any meat juices that have collected in the bowl and stir to combine. Add the thyme, stock, and radishes and stir. Place the lid over the pot, slightly askew so that some steam can escape, and bring to a low simmer. It's very important that the stew never boils; if it does, the meat will become tough. Cook until the radishes are tender, the meat is cooked through and very tender, and the broth has thickened, at least 1 hour.

5   Taste the broth for seasoning and add more salt, if desired. Stir in the yogurt, garnish with the parsley, and serve.

WINTER STEAK

with Sautéed Mushrooms

At the restaurant, I like to have different takes on popular dishes for different seasons. I love a simple Tuscan-style sliced steak, juicy and rare and topped with something intensely flavorful. In the fall and winter, I serve this pan-seared flank steak with a rich, velvety mushroom sauce enhanced with the browned bits from the pan and some of the meat juices themselves.

1   Preheat the oven to 400°F (205°C). Let the steak sit out until it comes to roughly room temperature; this will help it cook more evenly.

2   Season each side of the steak with ½ teaspoon of the salt and a very generous amount of pepper.

3   In a large ovenproof frying pan, preferably cast iron, heat the grapeseed oil over high heat until very hot, about 5 minutes. Place the steak in the pan and cook until nicely browned, about 3 minutes. Flip and cook until the other side is browned as well, about 2 minutes. Remove from the heat.

4   If you have some extra rosemary and thyme sprigs, toss a few into the pan. Transfer the pan to the oven and cook for 5 minutes for medium-rare.

5   Return the pan to the stovetop; transfer the steak to a plate to rest. (Be careful—the pan will be very hot.) To the pan, add the butter and olive oil and cook over medium-high heat until bubbling and melted, about 1 minute.

6   Add the shallots and garlic and stir. Add the chopped rosemary and the thyme and cook, stirring and scraping up the browned bits from the bottom of the pan, until the shallots are soft and slightly browned, about 2 minutes.

7   Add the mushrooms, a scant ½ teaspoon salt, and pepper to taste. Cook, stirring often, until softened and slightly browned, 2 to 3 minutes.

8   Pour the juices that have collected in the steak plate into the pan and stir. Add the wine and cook, stirring, until most of the liquid has cooked off, about 1 minute. Remove from the heat.

9   Cut the meat against the grain into slices ½ inch (12 millimeters) thick and arrange on a platter. Spoon the warm mushrooms over the steak. Sprinkle with parsley, if desired, and serve.

Serves 4

1 (1½-pound / 680-gram) piece flank steak, 1 inch (2.5 centimeters) thick

1½ scant teaspoons kosher salt, divided

Freshly ground black pepper

1 tablespoon grapeseed oil (or vegetable oil)

3 tablespoons (45 grams) unsalted butter

2 tablespoons extra-virgin olive oil

2 shallots, finely minced

2 cloves garlic, very thinly sliced

2 teaspoons very finely chopped fresh rosemary (from about 4 sprigs)

2 teaspoons fresh thyme leaves (from 4 to 5 sprigs)

8 ounces (225 grams) shiitake mushrooms, stems removed, cut into ¼-inch (6-millimeter) thick slices

8 ounces (225 grams) oyster mushrooms, 1 inch of thick stem removed, cut vertically into ¼-inch (6-millimeter) thick wedges

½ cup (120 milliliters) dry white wine

2 tablespoons roughly chopped fresh parsley (optional)

The first time I hosted a big Easter lunch at my apartment, I came up with a thematic and edible decorating scheme to fill out the table. Buy a variety of eggs in as many different shades and sizes as you can find. Look for pheasant, duck, and quail eggs as well as standard brown chicken eggs. If you have access to a farmers' market, you can often find local chicken eggs that are a lovely, unusual pale greenish blue. Hard-boil all the eggs separately according to size to avoid overcooking, and cool completely. Arrange them loosely along your table, mixing the different shapes in clusters around small bowls of celery salt. Your guests can peel and eat them over the course of the meal; the scattered remnants of the peeled shells have their own relaxed aesthetic charm.

SUMMER STEAK

with Sautéed Corn & Salsa

In the summer months at The Smile I serve our steak entrée arranged over a bed of sautéed plump, sweet corn and spoon a rustic tomato salsa on top.

1   *Make the salsa:* In a medium-size bowl, combine all the ingredients and let sit at room temperature while you prepare the steak and corn.

2   *Make the steak:* Preheat the oven to 400°F (205°C). Let the steak sit out until it comes to roughly room temperature; this will help it cook more evenly. Season each side of the steak with ½ teaspoon of the salt and a very generous amount of pepper.

3   In a large ovenproof frying pan, preferably cast iron, heat the grapeseed oil over high heat until very hot, about 3 minutes. Place the steak in the pan and cook until nicely browned, about 3 minutes. Flip and cook until the other side is browned as well, about 2 minutes.

4   Transfer the pan to the oven and cook for 5 minutes for medium-rare. Remove the steak to a carving board and let rest while you cook the corn.

5   *Make the corn:* In a wide heavy-bottomed sauté pan, heat the olive oil over medium-high heat for about 30 seconds. Add the scallions and cook until they are soft and some pieces are just beginning to brown, 2 to 3 minutes.

6   Add the corn kernels, salt, and pepper to taste. Cook, stirring often, until the corn is cooked through but not browned, about 4 minutes. Remove from the heat and stir in the lime zest.

7   Spread the corn on a platter. Cut the steak against the grain into pieces ½ inch (12 millimeters) thick. Arrange the steak over the corn. Spoon the salsa on top of the steak and serve.

Serves 4

FOR THE SALSA:

½ pint (150 grams) grape tomatoes, halved lengthwise

¼ large red onion, very finely diced

½ jalapeño pepper, seeded and very finely diced

½ cup (30 grams) roughly chopped fresh cilantro

½ teaspoon kosher salt

½ cup (120 milliliters) extra-virgin olive oil

2 tablespoons freshly squeezed lime juice (from 2 limes)

FOR THE STEAK:

1 (1½-pound / 680-gram) piece flank steak, 1 inch (2.5 centimeters) thick

1 teaspoon kosher salt

Freshly ground black pepper

1 tablespoon grapeseed oil (or vegetable oil)

FOR THE CORN:

3 tablespoons (45 milliliters) extra-virgin olive oil

1 small bunch scallions (about 6), roots trimmed, darkest green tops discarded, very thinly sliced

5 ears sweet yellow corn, shucked, kernels cut off as close to the cobs as possible (4 to 5 cups / 660 to 825 grams)

½ teaspoon kosher salt

Freshly ground black pepper

Grated zest of 2 limes

BALSAMIC ROASTED CHICKEN

Serves 4

3 cups (720 milliliters) balsamic vinegar (use the most inexpensive brand you can find)

1½ cups (360 milliliters) extra-virgin olive oil

2 large shallots, roughly chopped

1 bunch fresh thyme (about 25 sprigs)

4 cloves garlic

2 (3-pound / 1.4-kilogram) whole young chickens

2 teaspoons kosher salt

Freshly ground black pepper

1 teaspoon unsalted butter

We've had this roasted chicken on the menu at the restaurant since we first opened for dinner, and I always end up eating it at my personal staff meal. Intuitively, I would think that soaking chicken in a vat of vinegar would make it too sour, but the balsamic soaks into the skin in such a way that it becomes sweet and crisp when cooked. The pan juices are infused with thyme and a rich balsamic flavor that makes a simple, delicious sauce when reduced.

1   In a large, deep container, combine the vinegar, oil, shallots, and half the thyme.

2   Take each clove of garlic and press on it with the flat side of a chef's knife until it's cracked but still in one piece. Add to the marinade.

3   Rinse the chickens and pat them dry, then add them to the marinade, breast side down. They should be almost completely submerged.

4   Cover and refrigerate for at least 3 hours, turning once to make sure both sides are evenly soaked. The longer they marinate, the more intense the flavor will be, so if you have time, leave them overnight.

5   Preheat the oven to 400°F (205°C). Line a baking sheet or roasting pan with aluminum foil.

6   Remove the chickens from the marinade and dry well with paper towels. Discard the marinade. Season all sides of the chicken with the salt and a generous amount of pepper.

7   Place the remaining thyme sprigs in the prepared pan and arrange the chickens on top. Roast until the chickens are nicely browned and the juices run clear when you insert a knife into the deepest part of the thigh, about 1 hour. Set aside on a platter while you prepare the *jus*.

8   Pour the pan juices into a fat separator if you have one; if not, pour them into a container and let sit for a minute. Spoon off and discard the clear fat that rises to the top. Place the remaining juices in a saucepan. Bring to a boil and cook until reduced by about half, 2 to 3 minutes.

9   Add the butter and remove from the heat. Swirl the pan until the butter is melted. Drizzle the sauce over the chickens and serve.

CHICKEN PAILLARD

with Kalamata Olives, Capers & Lemon

Chicken paillard is the only way I really like cooking boneless, skinless chicken breast. Pounding the meat very thinly results in more surface area and a higher flavor-to-meat ratio in each bite. This is my quick-cooking, one-pan, last-minute dinner standby. No hidden tricks or subtle notes here—just bold, salty southern Italian flavors.

Serves 4

4 (4- to 6-ounce / 115- to 170-gram) boneless, skinless chicken breasts

2 teaspoons kosher salt

Freshly ground black pepper

4 tablespoons (60 milliliters) extra-virgin olive oil, divided

¼ teaspoon red chili flakes

1 bay leaf

3 cloves garlic, sliced lengthwise as thinly as possible

¼ cup (60 milliliters) freshly squeezed lemon juice (from 2 large lemons)

1 cup (180 grams) pitted kalamata olives, halved lengthwise

2 tablespoons drained capers

¼ cup (15 grams) roughly chopped fresh parsley

1   Place 1 chicken breast between two large pieces of parchment paper on a sturdy work surface. Pound with a meat mallet until the breast is about ¼ inch (6 millimeters) thick. If you don't have a mallet, you can use a heavy pan or rolling pin. Set aside and repeat with the remaining breasts.

2   Season each breast with ¼ teaspoon salt per side and a generous amount of pepper.

3   In your widest sauté or frying pan, heat 2 tablespoons (30 milliliters) of the oil, the chili flakes, and bay leaf until very hot, about 1 minute.

4   Place 2 of the breasts in the pan and cook until golden, 2 to 3 minutes. Flip and cook until the other side is also golden, 1 to 2 minutes. Transfer the breasts to a plate. Remove and discard the bay leaf. Repeat with the remaining 2 breasts and set aside. Remove the pan from the heat.

5   Add the remaining 2 tablespoons (30 milliliters) oil and the garlic to the pan. Reduce the heat to medium and cook until the garlic begins to soften, scraping up the browned bits from the bottom of the pan, about 1 minute.

6   Add the lemon juice and cook, stirring, for 30 seconds. Add the olives and capers and cook until well combined, about 1 minute.

7   Return the chicken and any juices from the plate to the pan. Stir to coat, cover, and cook until the chicken is completely cooked through, about 3 minutes.

8   Uncover, remove from the heat, and add the parsley. To serve, place each breast on a plate, or all of them on a platter, and spoon some of the olive mixture on top of each one.

MOROCCAN CHICKEN

with Preserved Lemon & Olives

Serves 4

4 skin-on, bone-in, split chicken breasts, or 1 large whole chicken, wings trimmed, cut into 8 pieces

2 teaspoons kosher salt, or more to taste

Freshly ground black pepper

2 tablespoons extra-virgin olive oil

1 large yellow onion, halved and thinly sliced

2 cloves garlic, roughly chopped

½ cup (30 grams) roughly chopped fresh cilantro, plus more for garnish

½ cup (30 grams) roughly chopped fresh parsley

1 teaspoon ground ginger

½ teaspoon ground cumin

¼ teaspoon crumbled saffron

3 cups (540 grams) cracked green Moroccan or Greek olives, not pitted (see Note)

2 halves preserved lemon (see page 36)

When I was growing up, every year on Christmas Day my parents would throw a big party for any friends and family who had nowhere else to go. My mother would make two enormous copper pots of this chicken and leave them bubbling on the stove all day. She used the recipe from Paula Wolfert's seminal cookbook *Mediterranean Cooking,* which now falls permanently open to the same page, stained from years of use. Gradually guests would fill the house, perching on the arms of sofas or sitting on the floor, balancing heavy plates of couscous and saucy chicken. The smell of olives and preserved lemons simmering on the stove always reminds me of the holidays and a kind of casual feast. This recipe is a simplification of Wolfert's, with fewer ingredients and steps, but the essence of the original remains.

In a pinch, if you can't find preserved lemons and don't have time to make them yourself, you can use regular lemons; the flavor won't be quite the same, but the dish will still be irresistible.

1   Rinse the chicken and thoroughly pat dry with paper towels. Season all sides with the 2 teaspoons salt and pepper to taste.

2   In a large heavy-bottomed pot, heat the oil over medium-high heat until very hot, 1 to 2 minutes.

3   Place the chicken breasts or pieces in the pot in a single layer, skin side down, working in batches if your pot isn't big enough. Cook until the skin is golden and crisp, 3 to 5 minutes. Flip and cook until the other side is also golden and crisp, 3 to 5 minutes. Transfer the chicken to a plate.

recipe continues

4   Reduce the heat to medium, add the onion and garlic, and stir well, scraping up the browned bits from the bottom of the pot. Cook until the onion has just softened, about 3 minutes.

5   Return the chicken to the pot. Add the cilantro, parsley, and 4 cups (960 milliliters) water.

6   Add the ginger, cumin, and saffron and stir. Bring to a simmer and cook, uncovered, for 20 minutes (the liquid needs to reduce slightly to intensify the flavor). If the chicken isn't completely covered by the liquid, turn the breasts or pieces occasionally so that both sides cook evenly.

7   Add the olives and preserved lemon and stir to combine. Cover and simmer until the chicken is very tender, at least 15 minutes more (but you can leave it on a low simmer for as long as you like). Season to taste with more salt and pepper, if desired. Garnish with cilantro and serve.

NOTE: If you can't find cracked Moroccan or Greek olives, any good-quality salty Mediterranean green olive will work.

CHEESE PLATE

Cheese is something of a miracle to me, and a testament to the power of process; I'm in awe of the fact that there are so many wildly different textures and flavors made from essentially the same basic ingredients: milk, salt, and rennet. I love tasting new cheeses, but it's easy to forget what you've tried and if and why you might have liked it. When I serve cheese to friends at home, I use this trick to let people know what they're eating: Arrange the cheeses on one long sheet of unbleached parchment paper and write the name, producer, milk type, and region of each cheese on the paper next to it. Serve cheese with your favorite bread or crackers and surround it with fresh fruit, nuts, and a jar of honey. When selecting cheese, the classic approach is to choose a range of milk types (at least one goat, one sheep, and one cow) and textures (creamy, chalky, semifirm, and very firm). However, one of the best cheese plates I ever had in my life was in a restaurant in a small town in Provence called La Celle. After dinner we were served three types of very fresh goat cheese because that's what was in season. All of them had the soft, lush grassiness of fresh goat's milk, but each had its own distinct character. Sometimes it can be more interesting to arrange a tasting of cheeses made with one kind of milk, or from one particular region—or even to try all that's available from one local farm.

CHICKEN PUTTANESCA

I borrowed this family recipe from a classmate at cooking school years ago, making a few changes along the way—I think she used fresh tomatoes, for example, but I find that good-quality canned crushed tomatoes have a comforting classic puttanesca taste. By itself this makes a great pasta sauce, but I make it so often that I created this version as a heartier dinner option. The flavor of the browned chicken gives the sauce a darker, meatier quality that I like.

1 Season both sides of the chicken pieces with the 2 teaspoons salt and pepper to taste.

2 In a large heavy-bottomed pot, heat the oil over medium-high heat until very hot, 1 to 2 minutes. Place the chicken pieces in the pot in a single layer and sear until golden brown on both sides, 3 to 5 minutes per side, working in batches if necessary. Transfer the chicken to a plate.

3 Reduce the heat to medium and add the onion, garlic, and anchovy paste to the pot. Cook, scraping up the browned bits from the bottom of the pot, until the onion is soft and translucent, 5 to 7 minutes.

4 Stir in the olives and capers and cook, stirring often, for 2 minutes. Add the wine and cook, uncovered, stirring occasionally, until most of the liquid is gone, about 5 minutes.

5 Add the tomatoes and stir to combine. Bring the sauce to a simmer. Add the chicken pieces and any juices to the pot; they should be just covered in sauce.

6 Cover, reduce the heat to low, and cook, uncovering and stirring occasionally, until the chicken is cooked through, at least 30 minutes. Season to taste with more salt and pepper, if desired, and serve.

Serves 4

1 (5-pound / 2.3-kilogram) chicken, wings trimmed, cut into 8 pieces

2 teaspoons kosher salt, or more to taste

Freshly ground black pepper

3 tablespoons (45 milliliters) extra-virgin olive oil

1 large yellow onion, diced into ½-inch (12-millimeter) pieces

2 cloves garlic, pressed or finely minced

1 teaspoon anchovy paste

1 cup (180 grams) pitted kalamata olives, roughly chopped

2 tablespoons drained capers

½ cup (120 milliliters) dry white wine

1 (28-ounce / 840-gram) can crushed tomatoes

HARISSA-&-HONEY-ROASTED TURKEY

Serves 8

¼ cup *harissa* paste

6 tablespoons (110 grams) forest honey (or the darkest honey you can find, such as chestnut or buckwheat)

2 tablespoons red wine

1 tablespoon extra-virgin olive oil

2 yellow onions, cut into ½-inch (12-millimeter) thick rounds

1 (12-pound / 5.5-kilogram) whole turkey

2 oranges

1 tablespoon kosher salt

Freshly ground black pepper

While it's true that most holidays have deeply rooted food traditions, Thanksgiving is the only one that is essentially just about the ritual of a big feast. I love that there are no obligations except to cook—or at the very least to eat. People are often fiercely nostalgic about their Thanksgiving meals (in my family, for example, it would constitute a serious breach of protocol if we decided to not make mashed yams with marshmallows, despite the fact that we also always make regular mashed potatoes). Though it wouldn't be Thanksgiving without some of our trademark side dishes, I actually like playing around with turkey recipes for a little variety from year to year. This Moroccan-inspired turkey is spicy, sweet, and very tender. The trick is that the honey in the marinade crisps the skin, trapping in the juices. The turkey will be almost blackened, which is why you have to brush the marinade on midway through cooking so it doesn't burn completely.

1 Preheat the oven to 425°F (220°C).

2 In a small bowl, combine the *harissa*, honey, wine, and oil and mix well.

3 Line the bottom of a roasting pan with the onion rounds.

4 Place the turkey in the sink. Remove and discard the neck and giblets from inside the cavity. Trim excess skin and fat from the neck and cavity openings. Rinse the turkey and thoroughly pat dry with paper towels.

5 Place the turkey on top of the onions and rub ¼ cup (60 milliliters) of the *harissa* mixture under the skin of the breast and around the leg joints.

6 Cut 1 of the oranges in half, stuff the cavity of the turkey with both halves, and tie the legs together with butcher's twine. Season all sides of the turkey with the salt and a generous amount of pepper.

7   Place the roasting pan on the lowest rack in the oven and roast for 15 minutes. Reduce the oven temperature to 350°F (175°C) and roast for an additional 45 minutes. If your turkey weighs more than 12 pounds (5.5 kilograms), add 10 minutes of cooking time for each extra pound (455 grams).

8   Remove the turkey from the oven and brush it all over with the remaining *harissa* mixture. Return it to the oven and roast for 1 hour, or until the juices run clear when a knife is inserted into the deepest part of the thigh.

9   Remove the turkey from the oven, baste with the pan juices, and let rest for 10 to 20 minutes.

10 Cut the remaining orange into rounds ½ inch (12 millimeters) thick and arrange them on a serving platter. Place the turkey on top. Pour off the remaining pan juices and melted onions and serve alongside the turkey.

I love the implied decadence of dessert. A simple dinner can seem like a feast when finished with a sugary homemade treat. While it obviously wouldn't be healthy to eat an enormous cake dripping with buttery icing every night, I think it's perfectly reasonable to indulge in a post-dinner delicacy every once in a while.

9
DESSERTS

I don't really separate the worlds of savory and sweet cooking. The same principles apply, but to a different palate of flavors. When I'm making dessert, I get to play with the natural acidic sweetness of fresh fruit, the darkly rich taste of brown sugar, and the intensely floral, slightly bitter depth of vanilla beans. Honey is by far my favorite sweet ingredient; as with wine, honey's flavor varies endlessly depending on the source and the season. The Greek honey I use has a wild and fresh thyme-infused golden flavor, while the honey that I buy from a farm in upstate New York tastes like apple blossoms and caramel. While sugar just adds sweetness to a dish, honey can add a whole dimension of flavors. Rose and orange-blossom waters are also great weapons in your dessert arsenal; they impart an indescribable, ephemeral aroma of far-off places. Made from the oils of pressed blossoms, flower waters are used throughout Middle Eastern and North African cooking, both in sweet and savory dishes. To the Western palate, unaccustomed to consuming anything so floral, they can seem too perfume-y. I use them sparingly—a drop of orange-blossom water to contrast with the bittersweet taste of crushed almonds, an almost undetectable splash of rose water to round out a red-wine-and-tangerine gelatin. Tasting the distillate of fresh flowers on the tongue is almost like inhaling them more intensely; it leaves me with the odd sensation that I'm still chasing a sublime, unattainable flowery flavor.

There seems to be an unspoken rule that if you're a serious cook, you can't enjoy baking. So many times I've heard professional chefs and food writers essentially say that baking is just not for them. Their argument is that you can't interact with the process in the same way, and instead of tasting, seasoning, and adjusting at every step, you're locked into the recipe; once it goes in the oven, you sit back and hope you've done everything right. And in the male-dominated world of professional cooking, there is the insidious sexist connotation that pastry is indelibly feminine and therefore a lesser form of cooking. The old stereotypes characterize the female pastry chef as precise, timid, and exacting, while a male chef is brash, forward, loud, and impulsive.

While I don't consider myself an avid baker, I think it's a shame for anyone to turn his or her back on the unique pleasure of producing a freshly homemade cake. Not all baking has to be about finicky doughs and exact measurements. The recipes here have a natural looseness to them. You can eyeball the ingredients for the top of the rhubarb crumble and still end up with an irresistible golden-brown cakiness that contrasts perfectly with the warm, tart rhubarb. And of course you don't have to bake to have a unique and satisfying dessert. By far my favorite desserts to prepare are roasted, poached, or stewed fruits; I love the way the added sweetness intensifies each fruit's distinct flavor. And best of all, they take very little time and effort and always look beautiful on the table.

Me at around age three, my mom, my sister, and OUR DOG, CHOOCHOO, in the garden of the house in Kamini

ALMOND COOKIES

with Bitter-Orange Glaze

In my romanticized memories, the air in Marrakech smells like orange blossoms and almonds, a blend of Creamsicle sweetness and sophisticated bitterness. The pairing of the two flavors is quintessentially Moroccan, popular in both savory and sweet dishes. These delicately spiced almond-based cookies are finished with an icing that combines the aroma of orange blossoms and the more intense kick of orange zest. As a bonus, they are gluten free, as well as quick and easy to make.

1 *Make the cookies:* Preheat the oven to 350°F (175°C). Line a baking sheet with parchment paper.

2 Place the almonds and almond extract in a food processor and process until they resemble bread crumbs, about 40 seconds. In a large bowl, combine the almond mixture, salt, cinnamon, and nutmeg and stir.

3 In a separate bowl, combine the egg whites, confectioners' sugar, and vanilla extract. Whisk until well combined. Pour the egg-white mixture into the almond mixture and stir until well combined.

4 Roll the mixture into roughly 1½-inch (4-centimeter) balls (about the size of ping-pong balls) and place them in rows on the prepared baking sheet, leaving about 1 inch (2.5 centimeters) between cookies. Using the bottom of a glass, press down lightly on each cookie so that it is about 2 inches (5 centimeters) in diameter and ½ inch (12 millimeters) thick.

5 Bake on the middle rack of the oven until the bottoms and edges of the cookies are just slightly golden, about 10 minutes. They should still be a bit chewy in the center. Let the cookies cool completely while you make the glaze.

6 *Make the glaze:* In a small bowl, combine all the ingredients and stir until smooth.

7 Spoon about 1 teaspoon glaze on top of each cookie and spread it evenly. Let the glaze sit untouched until it sets. The cookies can be stored in a cool, dry place, in a covered container, for up to 2 days.

Makes 20

FOR THE COOKIES:

2 cups (286 grams) whole blanched almonds

½ teaspoon almond extract

¼ teaspoon salt

¼ teaspoon ground cinnamon

⅛ teaspoon ground nutmeg

3 large egg whites

6 tablespoons (35 grams) confectioners' sugar

½ teaspoon vanilla extract

FOR THE GLAZE:

½ cup plus 2 tablespoons (65 grams) confectioners' sugar

2 tablespoons freshly squeezed orange juice (from ½ an orange)

1 teaspoon orange zest (from 1 large orange)

¼ teaspoon orange-blossom water

ALMOND CREAM

with Cherries & Pistachios

Serves 4

½ cup (120 milliliters) heavy cream

¼ cup (25 grams) confectioners' sugar

2 cups (500 grams) plain Greek yogurt (full-fat or 2%)

1 tablespoon almond liqueur, such as Disaronno, or 2 teaspoons almond extract

20 sour cherries in light syrup (from a 15-ounce / 430-gram jar)

½ cup (50 grams) shelled pistachios, roughly chopped

¼ cup (73 grams) good-quality honey

This almond-scented faux custard is a quick, no-cook dessert that still evokes exotic glamour. The whipped cream lightens the yogurt for a cloudlike, fluffy texture. To be honest, I think there's something to be said for the sticky sweetness—as well as the ease—of store-bought jarred sour cherries, but if cherries are in season, you can make your own fresh cherries in syrup: In a saucepan, combine 2 cups pitted cherries, ¼ cup sugar, a splash of water, and a squeeze of lemon juice and cook until the liquid is syrupy but the cherries haven't fallen apart, about 5 minutes.

1   In a medium-size mixing bowl, using an electric beater, whip the cream and confectioners' sugar together until soft peaks form.

2   Add the yogurt and almond liqueur and whip until smooth. (At this point you can refrigerate the mixture, covered, for up to 1 day.)

3   Divide the almond cream among four dessert bowls or glasses. Top each with 5 cherries, sprinkle with the pistachios, and drizzle with the honey.

ELEGANT DESSERT

A family friend hosts a party at her apartment on the Upper East Side every Christmas Eve. After a buffet dinner, for dessert she passes around a tray of peeled clementines and almond-chocolate clusters. This has always struck me as the height of elegance, the perfect thing after a big meal—just a taste of rich, sweet chocolate and a palate-cleansing burst of citrus. Buy a box or two of clementines and peel them, cover the peeled fruit with a damp paper towel, and keep refrigerated. Buy an assortment of good-quality chocolate bars with cocoa contents varying from very dark to milk, and break them unevenly into large pieces. Serve the clementines piled in a clean white bowl and arrange the chocolate on a silver tray or platter.

BERRIES & CREAM

Serves 4

FOR THE VANILLA CREAM:

1½ cups (360 milliliters) good-quality
   heavy cream

2 tablespoons sugar

1 vanilla bean, split

FOR THE BERRIES:

1 pound (455 grams) fresh strawberries,
   rinsed, hulled, and cut in half (or
   quartered if large)

½ pint (170 grams) raspberries

½ pint (190 grams) blueberries

2 tablespoons sugar

1 teaspoon balsamic vinegar

This is a simple dessert perfect for summertime, when fresh berries are plump and flavorful. Infusing the cream with a vanilla bean gives it a unique fragrance and appealing little flecks of tiny black vanilla seeds.

1   *Make the vanilla cream:* In a small saucepan, combine the cream and sugar. Gently scrape the inside of the vanilla bean with a paring knife and toss the seeds and pod into the pan.

2   Heat over low heat, stirring often, until the sugar is dissolved and the vanilla has infused the cream, about 4 minutes. Remove from the heat just when the mixture starts to simmer.

3   Let cool completely, then transfer the mixture to a pitcher or container and refrigerate. I like to keep the vanilla bean in as long as possible to continue to infuse the cream with flavor.

4   *Make the berries:* In a bowl, combine the berries, sugar, and vinegar and stir to coat. Let sit at room temperature until the sugar has dissolved and the berries are juicy, about 5 minutes. (At this point you can refrigerate the berries until you're ready to serve them.)

5   Divide the berries among four bowls. Remove the vanilla bean from the cream and discard. Stir the cream and bring the pitcher to the table. Let your diners pour the cream over the berries as they like.

GOAT-CHEESE CAKE

with Blood-Orange Marmalade

The slightly grassy flavor the goat cheese adds to this creamy cake, combined with the bold citrus and honey marmalade, reminds me of a Spanish cheese plate.

1 *Make the cake:* Preheat the oven to 325°F (165°C). Butter a round cake pan, 9 inches (23 centimeters) wide by 2 inches (5 centimeters) deep.

2 In a bowl (or in the bowl of a stand mixer), combine the crème fraîche, eggs, sugar, and vanilla extract. Beat with an electric beater (or stand mixer) on medium speed until smooth and well combined.

3 Add the goat cheese a bit at a time and beat on medium speed until all the cheese is incorporated. Mix until completely smooth.

4 Pour the batter into the prepared pan. Place the pan inside a large rectangular baking dish. Pour water into the larger dish until it reaches halfway up the outside of the cake pan. Bake until the cake is completely set and slightly browned on top, about 50 minutes.

5 Remove from the oven and remove the cake pan from the water bath. Let the cake cool in the pan; it will shrink away from the sides as it cools.

6 Place a large plate on top of the cake pan and invert it. Remove the pan; the cake should come out easily. Refrigerate until completely chilled and firm.

7 *Make the marmalade:* Using a strip zester, zest 2 of the oranges. If you don't have a strip zester, use a paring knife to remove only the orange part of the skin, then cut it into very long, thin strips and set them aside.

8 Cut both ends off of all the oranges. Using a paring knife, follow the curve of the fruit to remove the peel and white pith.

9 Working over a bowl to catch the juices, use a paring knife to cut out the fruit segments from the membrane and place them in the bowl, then squeeze the juice out of and discard the membranes.

10 Place the zest, segments, and juice in a heavy-bottomed saucepan. Add the sugar and honey and bring to a simmer over medium-high heat. Cook, stirring occasionally, until the liquid is reduced and syrupy, about 15 minutes. Remove from the heat and let cool completely.

11 Gently spread the marmalade in a thin layer over the entire top of the cake and serve.

Serves 8

FOR THE CAKE:

Unsalted butter for the pan

1 cup (250 grams) crème fraîche or sour cream

3 large eggs

½ cup (100 grams) sugar

2 teaspoons vanilla extract

1 pound (455 grams) soft goat cheese, at room temperature

FOR THE MARMALADE:

4 blood oranges

¼ cup (50 grams) sugar

2 tablespoons honey

APRICOT "EGG" PAVLOVAS

I don't always have the patience to make a complicated dessert. When I do have the urge to impress, I go for these elegant egg-shaped treats, a classic combination of meringue, cream, and fruit. While there are a few steps to the recipe, each is fairly simple unto itself, and everything can be made in advance and assembled right before serving. I think of this as an exercise in layering different levels of sweetness and texture: the airy, lightly sweet meringue and velvety whipped cream topped with the decadent, syrupy poached apricots. The fruit and whipped cream on their own make a lovely simpler version if you don't want to go all-out fancy.

1   *Make the meringues:* Preheat the oven to 300°F (150°C). Line a baking sheet with parchment paper.

2   In a medium-size bowl, using an electric beater, beat the egg whites until soft peaks form. Gradually beat in the confectioners' sugar, granulated sugar, cream of tartar, and almond extract. Beat until stiff peaks form and the meringue is very white and glossy.

3   Using two large spoons, scoop 6 dollops (about ⅓ cup / 30 grams each) of the meringue onto the prepared baking sheet and shape them into roughly 2-by-3-inch (5-by-7.5-centimeter) ovals. Using the back of a spoon, make a slight indentation in the center of each oval.

4   Place the meringues in the oven and immediately reduce the oven temperature to 200°F (90°C). Bake until stiff, about 2 hours. Remove from the oven and let cool completely. (Once cool, the meringues can be stored in an airtight container overnight.)

recipe continues

Makes 6

FOR THE MERINGUES:

2 large egg whites

¼ cup (25 grams) confectioners' sugar

¼ cup (50 grams) granulated sugar

¼ teaspoon cream of tartar

½ teaspoon almond extract

FOR THE POACHED APRICOTS:

1 (375-milliliter) half bottle of Sauternes or any good white dessert wine (about 1½ cups)

½ cup (100 grams) granulated sugar

2 tablespoons unsalted butter

3 ripe apricots, halved and pitted

FOR THE WHIPPED CREAM:

½ cup (120 milliliters) heavy cream

1 tablespoon confectioners' sugar

¼ teaspoon vanilla extract

5   *Make the poached apricots:* In a medium-size saucepan, combine the wine, sugar, and butter and bring to a simmer over medium heat.

6   Add the apricots and simmer until they are tender but still hold their shape, about 4 minutes. Using a slotted spoon, transfer the apricots to a bowl.

7   Increase the heat and bring the sauce to a boil. Cook until the liquid is reduced by half, about 5 minutes. Remove from the heat. (The apricots and sauce can be refrigerated separately, covered, and reheated just before serving.)

8   *Make the whipped cream:* In a medium-size bowl, using an electric beater, whip the cream, sugar, and vanilla extract together until soft peaks form. (The whipped cream can be refrigerated, covered, for up to 1 day.)

9   Assemble six dessert plates and place 1 meringue on each. Spoon about 2 tablespoons of the whipped cream in the center of each meringue. Top with an apricot half, cut side down, drizzle with the poaching liquid, and serve.

GREEK-YOGURT PANNA COTTA

with Warm Lemon-Honey Sauce

During the summers in Greece, I always start my morning with a bowl of dense, creamy Greek yogurt topped with generous amounts of golden honey. With this recipe, I wanted to take the spirit of those flavors and transform them into a slightly more refined dessert.

1   Place the milk in a medium-size saucepan, add the gelatin, and let stand for 1 minute. Whisk in the cream, sugar, and salt.

2   With a paring knife, gently scrape the seeds of the vanilla bean into the saucepan, then throw in the pod. Heat the mixture over medium heat, whisking constantly, until it comes to a boil.

3   Remove from the heat and whisk in the yogurt.

4   Pour the mixture into four to six roughly 8-ounce (240-milliliter) ramekins, or any small cups or containers that work. Refrigerate until set, at least 2 hours.

5   To remove the panna cottas, dip each ramekin or container into a shallow bowl of very hot water, being careful not to splash the top of the dessert. Gently run a sharp paring knife around the edge of the panna cotta. Invert the ramekin or container onto a dessert plate and lift it up; the panna cotta should slide out easily.

6   In a small saucepan, heat the honey and lemon juice over medium heat until the mixture comes to a simmer. Cook until slightly reduced, about 1 minute.

7   Spoon about 1 tablespoon warm sauce over each panna cotta and serve.

Makes 4 to 6

1 cup (240 milliliters) whole milk

1 envelope unflavored gelatin

1 cup (240 milliliters) heavy cream

½ cup (100 grams) sugar

Pinch of salt

½ vanilla bean, split

1½ cups (375 grams) full-fat plain Greek yogurt

¼ cup (73 grams) good-quality honey

2 tablespoons freshly squeezed lemon juice (from 1 large lemon)

STICKY-TOFFEE DATE PUDDING

Serves 6 to 8

FOR THE CAKE:

1 cup (170 grams) tightly packed pitted dates, roughly chopped

½ cup tightly packed (80 grams) pitted prunes, roughly chopped

½ cup (1 stick / 115 grams) unsalted butter, softened, plus more for the pan

½ cup (110 grams) dark brown sugar

2 large eggs

½ cup (170 grams) date molasses

1 teaspoon vanilla extract

1 teaspoon ground ginger

1½ cups (185 grams) all-purpose flour

2 teaspoons baking powder

¼ teaspoon salt

FOR THE STICKY-TOFFEE SAUCE:

½ cup (1 stick / 115 grams) unsalted butter

1 cup (240 milliliters) heavy cream

½ cup (110 grams) dark brown sugar

½ cup (170 grams) date molasses

2 teaspoons vanilla extract

¼ teaspoon salt

In my version of the classic English dessert, which features soaked chopped dates mixed into the batter, I've replaced some of the sugar with date molasses to emphasize the rich flavor and natural sweetness of the dates. You can buy date molasses at specialty shops or order it online; it can be used as an exotic alternative to sugar, regular molasses, or maple syrup. I love how the rich, gooey caramel sauce combines with the spice notes in the cake for a decadent, comforting winter dessert. This would also pair nicely with cardamom whipped cream (see page 226) or a big scoop of vanilla ice cream.

1   *Make the cake:* Preheat the oven to 350°F (175°C). Butter a round cake pan, 8 inches (20 centimeters) in diameter by 2 inches (5 centimeters) deep.

2   In a small bowl, combine the dates and prunes and cover with boiling water (for a kick you can add a splash of cognac or brandy). Let them soak while you prepare the rest of the cake, about 15 minutes.

3   In a large mixing bowl, using an electric beater, beat the butter and brown sugar together until fluffy. Add the eggs, one at a time, beating after each addition to incorporate. Add the date molasses, vanilla extract, and ginger and beat to combine.

4   In a separate bowl, stir together the flour, baking powder, and salt. Add the flour mixture to the egg mixture a bit at a time, beating after each addition, until well combined.

5   Drain the dates and prunes in a fine-mesh strainer. Press on them with a spoon to get rid of excess liquid. Add them to the batter and stir with a spoon.

6   Pour the batter into the prepared pan and bake until a toothpick inserted into the center comes out clean, 45 to 50 minutes.

7   *Meanwhile, make the sticky-toffee sauce:* In a medium-size saucepan, melt the butter over medium heat. Stir in the cream, brown sugar, date molasses, vanilla extract, and salt. Bring to a gentle simmer and cook, stirring, until reduced by half, about 3 minutes.

8   Let the cake cool in the pan until just warm. Place a plate on top of the cake pan, invert it, and remove the pan. Using another plate, invert the cake again so it's right side up. Using a toothpick or skewer, poke holes all over the top of the cake, going almost all the way through. Cover the cake with half of the warm sauce, pouring and spreading slowly, allowing the cake to absorb the liquid. Let sit for at least 20 minutes.

9   Just before serving, reheat the remaining sauce and reduce until slightly thicker, about 1 minute. Spoon more sauce on top of the cake. Bring a bowl of any remaining sauce to the table and serve.

LEMON & OLIVE OIL POUND CAKE

Makes 1 standard-size pound cake

FOR THE CAKE:

Unsalted butter for the pan

2½ cups (310 grams) all-purpose flour, sifted, plus more for the pan

2 teaspoons baking powder

¼ teaspoon salt

1 cup (200 grams) sugar

2 large eggs

½ cup (120 milliliters) extra-virgin olive oil

½ cup (120 milliliters) whole milk

Grated zest of 1 lemon

¼ cup (60 milliliters) freshly squeezed lemon juice (from 2 large lemons)

½ teaspoon vanilla extract

FOR THE GLAZE:

½ cup (50 grams) confectioners' sugar, sifted

2 tablespoons freshly squeezed lemon juice (from 1 large lemon)

2 teaspoons extra-virgin olive oil

Extra-virgin olive oil is my default for cooking: There's always a big can of it by my stovetop that I run through at an alarmingly fast pace. Mostly it's a means to an end, a backdrop for whatever other ingredients I'm using. Sometimes it's nice to make something, like this fluffy lemon cake, that showcases the distinct, fruity aroma of a nice olive oil. For good measure I use a little more oil in the glaze to give it an added layer of raw flavor. You can serve this as a dessert or with a strong cup of coffee as a breakfast cake.

1   *Make the cake:* Preheat the oven to 350°F (175°C). Grease an 8½-by-4½-inch (21.5-by-11-centimeter) loaf pan with butter and dust with flour.

2   In a medium-size bowl, combine the flour, baking powder, and salt. In a separate large bowl, whisk together the sugar, eggs, oil, milk, zest, juice, and vanilla extract.

3   Add the dry ingredients to the wet ingredients and mix well with a rubber spatula, making sure there are no lumps. Pour into the prepared pan. Smooth the top and bake until a toothpick inserted into the center comes out clean, about 50 minutes. Let cool slightly, then remove from the pan and let cool completely.

4   *Make the glaze:* In a small bowl, combine all the ingredients and mix well. Spoon the glaze over the top of the cake. Let the glaze set, then serve.

PEARS POACHED IN GREEK WINE

My mom always used to make these for dinner parties when I was a child. The throw-it-in-the-pot ease and elegance of whole pears dyed a dark-wine crimson appealed to her artist's sensibility. They can be made up to two days in advance and refrigerated, covered in their poaching liquid. The longer they marinate, the richer their flavor and the more intense their color will become.

1 Peel the pears, leaving the stems attached.

2 In a medium-size saucepan, combine the remaining ingredients and 2 cups (480 milliliters) water. Place over medium heat, add the pears (they should be just covered with the liquid), and bring to a simmer.

3 Cook, uncovered, until the pears are completely tender, about 20 minutes. Turn with a spoon occasionally to make sure they are evenly cooked.

4 Let cool completely in the saucepan, then transfer the pears and some of the poaching liquid to a serving bowl. The pears can also be refrigerated overnight in the poaching liquid and either served cold or reheated.

Serves 4

4 Bartlett pears (or any other large sweet, firm pears)

1 (750-milliliter) bottle of inexpensive Greek sweet red wine, such as Mavrodaphne (about 3 cups)

½ cup (100 grams) sugar

½ cup (145 grams) honey

2 cinnamon sticks

2 strips lemon zest, each 1 by 2 inches (2.5 by 5 centimeters)

1 vanilla bean, split

CHERRY VA...

PEACH

PISTACHIO

CHOCOLATE CHIP

EMON LIME SHERBET

STRAWBERRY

BUTTER PECAN

RHUBARB CRUMBLE

with Cardamom Cream

Serves 4 to 6

FOR THE CARDAMOM CREAM:

1 cup (240 milliliters) heavy cream

2 tablespoons confectioners' sugar

½ teaspoon ground cardamom

½ teaspoon vanilla extract

FOR THE FILLING:

1 pound (455 grams) rhubarb, ends trimmed, cut into ½-inch pieces

8 ounces (225 grams) strawberries, hulled and halved

½ cup (100 grams) granulated sugar

1 vanilla bean, split

¼ cup (60 milliliters) orange juice

1 green-skinned pear, cored and grated (including the skin)

FOR THE TOPPING:

¾ cup (90 grams) all-purpose flour

½ cup (110 grams) light brown sugar

½ cup (40 grams) rolled oats

½ teaspoon kosher salt

¼ teaspoon ground nutmeg

½ cup (1 stick / 115 grams) very cold unsalted butter

Rhubarb crumble is my favorite classic American dessert—less fussy than a pie, with a sweet, tart, gooey filling and an irresistible buttery-crisp layer on top. The hint of cardamom in the whipped cream gives it a subtle kick of exotic spice.

1   *Make the cardamom cream:* In a mixing bowl, combine all the ingredients and whip with an electric beater until stiff peaks form. Refrigerate, covered, until ready to use (for up to one day).

2   Preheat the oven to 350°F (175°C).

3   *Make the filling:* Place the rhubarb, strawberries, granulated sugar, vanilla bean, and orange juice in a saucepan. Cook, stirring occasionally, over medium-high heat until the juices are beginning to run but the rhubarb still holds its shape, about 5 minutes.

4   Remove from the heat and stir in the pear. Discard the vanilla bean and transfer the mixture to a 9-inch (23-centimeter) ceramic or heatproof glass pie dish. Let cool while you prepare the topping.

5   *Make the topping:* In a medium-size bowl, combine the flour, brown sugar, rolled oats, salt, and nutmeg. Mix together until well combined. Cut the butter into small pieces and add it to the flour mixture. Rub the mixture together with your fingers until the butter is incorporated and the mixture has a crumbly texture.

6   Sprinkle the topping over the filling. Place the pie dish on a baking sheet (in case the filling drips out the sides) and bake on the middle rack of the oven until the topping is dark golden and the rhubarb is bubbling, about 1 hour.

7   Serve warm alongside a bowl of the cardamom cream.

ROSEMARY- & -HONEY- ROASTED QUINCE

Quince have a lovely, intense fruity aroma. A bowl of them ripening on your kitchen table will slowly perfume the whole room with the scent of roses and honey. Though inedible when raw, the fruit is dense and flavorful when cooked, with a beautiful golden pink color. This is my favorite way to eat quince, slow-roasted with a few sprigs of rosemary, some wine, butter, and honey. The fruit pairs beautifully with vanilla ice cream.

1 Preheat the oven to 350°F (175°C).

2 Place the rosemary sprigs in an 8-by-11-inch (20-by-28-centimeter) baking dish. Place the quince halves on top, cut sides up. Pour the wine over the quince. Squeeze the lemon and drizzle the honey on top.

3 Place ½ tablespoon butter on each quince half and sprinkle with nutmeg. Cover tightly with aluminum foil and poke a few holes in the top with a fork.

4 Roast for 1 hour. Take the dish out of the oven and remove the foil. Spoon the juices over the quince and return to the oven. Cook, uncovered, until they are completely tender, have turned a rose-pink color, and are slightly golden brown on top, about 45 more minutes.

5 Serve with the syrupy cooking juices.

Serves 4 to 6

2 sprigs fresh rosemary

4 quince (about 2 pounds / 910 grams), peeled, halved, and cored

1 (375-milliliter) half bottle of white dessert wine (about 1½ cups)

Juice of ½ lemon

¼ cup (73 grams) honey

4 tablespoons (½ stick / 50 grams) unsalted butter, cut into ½-tablespoon pieces

⅛ teaspoon ground nutmeg

SANGRIA GELATIN

Serves 6

1 cup (240 milliliters) ginger ale

2 envelopes unflavored gelatin

1 cup (240 milliliters) full-bodied, fruity Spanish red wine, such as Rioja

1 cup (240 milliliters) tangerine juice

½ cup (100 grams) sugar

½ teaspoon rose water

½ pint (170 grams) raspberries

My maternal grandmother almost never cooked, a rarity for women in her generation. She had a full-time job working in child-welfare services and spent any free time she had in nature, fishing, camping, or hiking. She did have one "secret" recipe that she used to make for me when I was young—whenever she made Jell-O, she would use ginger ale instead of water. It may be partly nostalgia, but I love the way this method gives the finished dessert a bit of extra sweetness and a mild gingery note. It's a nice match here for the full-bodied wine and bold tangerine. I like to think of this as a sophisticated version of a Jell-O shot.

1   Place the ginger ale in a large bowl and sprinkle the gelatin on top. Let stand for 1 minute.

2   In a medium-size saucepan, combine the wine, tangerine juice, sugar, and rose water and bring to a boil.

3   Pour the wine mixture over the gelatin mixture and stir to combine.

4   Divide the raspberries among six wide-mouthed champagne glasses or dessert cups. Pour ½ cup of the gelatin mixture into each glass and refrigerate until firm, about 3 hours. Serve cold.

QUICK-STEWED PLUMS

Serves 4 to 6

4 black plums, sliced into 8 wedges each, pits discarded

Juice of ½ orange

¼ cup (55 grams) packed brown sugar

2 strips orange zest, each 1 by 2 inches (2.5 by 5 centimeters)

1 vanilla bean, split

Vanilla ice cream

I have a weakness for quick-cooked fruit desserts like this one. Planning in advance and making an elaborate cake can be very satisfying, but it's often more realistic to have a recipe on hand that you can throw together in minutes, especially if you've just cooked a full dinner. I love the way the pigment in the plums' skin infuses the cooking liquid, making for a vivid contrast with the vanilla ice cream. At the restaurant we serve a breakfast version of this dish—chilled, drizzled over Greek yogurt, and topped with crushed almonds.

1   In a medium-size saucepan, combine all the ingredients except the ice cream with ¼ cup (60 milliliters) water and heat over medium heat. Bring to a simmer and cook, stirring occasionally, until the plums are just falling apart, about 8 minutes.

2   Remove the plums from the heat and serve with their cooking liquid over bowls of the ice cream.

SPICED HOT CHOCOLATE

This hot chocolate is so rich and intensely chocolatey that I think it qualifies as a full-blown dessert. Use pure cocoa powder and good-quality baking chocolate for the best results. The hot liquid releases the oils in the orange-zest garnish, adding a note of bright flavor.

1   In a heavy-bottomed saucepan, whisk together the milk, sugar, cocoa powder, and spices. Bring to a boil over medium heat, whisking constantly.

2   Remove from the heat and stir in the vanilla extract and chocolate, whisking until the chocolate is completely melted and combined.

3   Using a paring knife or vegetable peeler, remove 4 strips, each 2 to 3 inches (5 to 7.5 centimeters) long, of the zest from the orange, leaving as much of the white pith behind as possible. Place 1 strip in each of four mugs.

4   Pour the hot chocolate over the orange zest into the mugs and serve.

NOTE: For the best results it's important to use high-quality 100 percent cacao cocoa powder, such as Valrhona, and the best baking chocolate you can find, such as Ghirardelli.

Serves 4

4 cups (960 milliliters) whole milk

6 tablespoons (75 grams) sugar

2 tablespoons unsweetened cocoa powder (100% cacao)

¼ teaspoon ground cinnamon

¼ teaspoon ground nutmeg

⅛ teaspoon ground cardamom

1 tablespoon vanilla extract

5 ounces (140 grams) good-quality unsweetened baking chocolate, chopped (see Note)

1 large orange

SUGGESTED MENUS

MEDITERRANEAN THANKSGIVING

Harissa-&-Honey-Roasted Turkey

Olive Oil Mashed Potatoes

Fennel, Cucumber & Pomegranate Salad

Rosemary-&-Honey-Glazed Carrots

Pears Poached in Greek Wine

FRENCH COUNTRYSIDE DINNER

Potato-Leek Soup

Balsamic Roasted Chicken

Lemony Roasted Potatoes with Grapes & Rosemary

String Beans with Lemon & Caramelized Shallots

Spiced Hot Chocolate

EASTER FEAST

Minted Lamb Roast

Sautéed Shaved Asparagus

Farfalle with Figs, Lemon & Dill

Mixed-Green Salad with Plums

Apricot "Egg" Pavlovas

SUMMER GRILL

Beet & Watermelon-Radish Salad with Buffalo Mozzarella

Peppery Grilled Rib Eye with Charred Scallions

Grilled Corn with Lime Butter

Spaghetti with Heirloom Cherry Tomatoes

Berries & Cream

Hibiscus Iced Tea

STEAK & POTATOES

Romaine Hearts with Buttermilk-Chive Dressing

Winter Steak with Sautéed Mushrooms

Sweet Potato Puree

Sweet & Spicy Sautéed Lacinato Kale

Rosemary-&-Honey-Roasted Quince

ASTORIA-STYLE *MEZZE*

Greek Fava: Yellow Split Pea Puree

Almond Dip

Roasted-Carrot Dip

Bruschetta

Pink Sangria

WINE & CHEESE

Pickled Kumquats

Pink Pickles

Marinated Mixed Olives

Marinated Goat Cheese with Fried Garlic & Sage

Assorted Cheeses

FALL DINNER

Squash, Blood Orange & Dandelion Greens

Brussels Sprouts with Bacon & Pomegranate Seeds

Pork & Cranberry Beans with Rosemary Butter

Quick-Stewed Plums

ITALIAN DINNER

Seared Fennel Wedges
with Orange Dressing

Chicken Puttanesca

Throw-It-in-the-Oven Garlic Bread

String Beans with Fried Shallots,
Pecorino & Basil

Greek-Yogurt Panna Cotta with
Warm Lemon-Honey Sauce

MELIA'S CHRISTMAS DINNER

Green Salad with Dill
& Lemon Dressing

Moroccan Chicken with
Preserved Lemon & Olives

Couscous with Currants & Pistachios

Vegetables in Spiced Broth
over Couscous

Sticky-Toffee Date Pudding

PLAIN & SIMPLE

Arugula Salad with Roasted
Grape Tomatoes

Zucchini Rounds Simmered in
Fresh Tomato Sauce

Stovetop Simmered Potatoes

Roasted Brook Trout with
Fennel Seeds

ORANGE BLOSSOMS & OLIVES

Parchment-Steamed Cod with
Olive-Orange *Gremolata*

Roasted Beets

Roasted Fairytale Eggplants
with Spicy Lime Yogurt Sauce

Almond Cookies with
Bitter-Orange Glaze

SPRING DINNER

Fava Bean Crostini

Butterhead Lettuce & Radish Salad

Rosemary & Oregano Pork Chops

Grilled Asparagus with
Preserved Lemon

Rhubarb Crumble with
Cardamom Cream

HYDRA TAVERNA

Tzatziki

Greek Island Salad

Stuffed Tomatoes

Boiled Dandelion Greens

Grilled Mediterranean *Dorade*
with Lemon-Oregano Oil

Almond Cream with
Cherries & Pistachios

GARDEN PARTY

Minted Snap Peas

Manchego & Sungold-Tomato-
Jam Sandwiches

Lime Shandies

Sangria Gelatin

ONE TWO BRUNCH

Frisée, Bacon, Date &
Quail-Egg Salad

Frittata

Lemon & Olive Oil
Pound Cake

COCKTAIL PARTY

Moroccan Champagne Cocktail

Fresh Fig, Honey & Basil Crostini

Spiced Candied Pistachios

ACKNOWLEDGMENTS

FIRST AND MOST IMPORTANTLY, I NEED TO THANK MY MOM for being an inspirational cook and raising me on such amazing food. I want to thank Meredith James for helping me develop so many of these recipes during our years catering together. Thanks to my husband, Frankie, for being the best taste tester and editor and my favorite person to eat dinner with. Thanks to my sister, Mirabelle, for always being so supportive. Thanks to my editor, Natalie Kaire, for helping me through the process from the beginning. Thanks to Lucy Schaeffer, Simon Andrews, and Amy Wilson for creating such beautiful images out of my recipes. Thanks to Jennifer Rubell for showing me the way and letting me copy all of her good ideas. Thanks to Maya Gurley for giving me the chance to learn in her restaurant and setting the standard for simple but delicious cooking. Finally, thanks to Matt Kliegman and Carlos Quirarte for trusting me to run The Smile's kitchen.

INDEX

Note: Page references in *italics* indicate photographs.